marques vickers

TWISTED TOUR GUIDE PORTLAND AND SALEM

SHOCKING DEATHS, SCANDALS AND VICE

By Marques Vickers

Editorial Assistance: Caroline Vickers

**MARQUIS PUBLISHING
TACOMA, WASHINGTON**

Copyright @2020-2023 Marques Vickers

Version 1.3

Published by Marquis Publishing
Tacoma, Washington
TwistedTourGuides.com

Vickers, Marques, 1957

TWISTED TOUR GUIDE PORTLAND AND SALEM
Shocking Deaths, Scandals and Vice

Dedication: To my daughters Charline and Caroline.

TABLE OF CONTENTS

SALEM

ABOUT THE AUTHOR

SOURCES AND ARCHIVES SOURCED

Sullivansgulch.org, NPR.org, DavidcampbellMemorial.org, PacificReporter.com, ArizonaRepublic.com, PublicHistoryPDX.org, Sipnorthwest.com, Hauntedrooms.com, Paddys.com, StatesmanJournal.com, GhostHauntedHouses.com, Waymarking.com, OregonPioneers.com , *Wicked Portland: The Wild and Lusty Underworld of a Frontier Seaport Town* by J. D. John, Portlandwaterfront.blogspot.com, Realcombatmedia.com Pamplinmedia.com, PortlandMercury.com, Steemit.com, LostOregon.org, TheSocietyHotel.com, *Portland's Lost Waterfront* by Barney Blalock, WillametteWeek.com, PDXMonthly.com, IdiotForJodie.com, Spokane Spokesman-Review, Department of Corrections: Washington State, *Murder & Scandal in Prohibition Portland* by JD Chandler and Theresa Griffen Kennedy, Portlandcrime.blogspot.com , The Skanner.com, *Portland on the Take: Mid-Century Crime Bosses, Civic Corruption & Forgotten Murders* by JD Chandler and JB Fisher, Portland City Telephone Directory, ORHistory.com, News.streetroots.org, ArchInform.net, Zaget.com, Issac.blogs.com, FindAGrave.com, CafeUnknown.com, Portland Evening Telegram, TheAwl.com, Tillamook Headlight Herald, Genealogytrails.com, *Murder and Mayhem in Portland, Oregon* by JD Chandler, Google Maps, CityLab.com, OSBar.org, Patch.com, News.Streetroots.org, Imbibe Magazine, OregonLive.com, OregonBusiness.com. OregonEncyclopediia.org, SerialKillerCalendar.com, *Hidden History of Portland Oregon* by JD Chandler, AllThatsInteresting.com, OSBar.org, *Same Sex Affairs: Constructing and Controlling Homosexuality in the Pacific Northwest* by Peter Boag, Morning Oregonian, FindAGrave.com, Brianhuntbooks.com, OffbeatOregon.com, Wikipedia.org, Gay & Lesbian

Archives of the Pacific Northwest (GLAPN.org), *Heroes and Rascals of Old Oregon* by J.D. John

Photography shot between 2019-2020. Some of the locations may have altered with time and ownership changes. Many of the locations are still privately inhabited. Please don't disturb the residents.

TWISTED TOUR GUIDE TO PORTLAND AND SALEM

Avoid The Tourist Herds.

What could be more uninspiring than seeing the identical attractions that everyone else has for decades?

This Twisted Tour Guide escorts you to the places locals don't want to talk about anymore...the same places people once couldn't stop talking about. Long after the screaming headlines and sensationalism has subsided, these bizarre, infamous and obscure historical sites remain hidden awaiting rediscovery.

Each visitation site in this guide is accompanied by a story. Many of the narratives defy believability, yet they are true. The profiled cast of characters feature saints and sinners (with emphasis towards the latter).

Notorious crimes, murders, accidental deaths, suicides, kidnappings, vice and scandal are captivating human interest tales. Paranormal activity in the aftermath is common.

The photography from each profile showcases the precise location where each event occurred. The scenes can seem ordinary, weird and sometimes very revealing towards clarifying the background behind events.

If you're seeking an alternative to conventional tourism, this Twisted Tourist Guide is ideal. Each directory accommodates the restless traveler and even resident looking for something unique and different. You will never imagine or scrutinize the Portland (Rose City) and Salem area through rose tinted glasses again.

PORTLAND

Spirits Evidenced at Portland's Famed Witches Castle

Forest Park's Balch Creek was initially part of a land claim established in 1850 by Danford Balch. The land track was extensive and Balch hired a transient worker named Mortimer Stump originally from Vancouver to help clear it.

Stump lived with Balch's family for a few years consisting of his wife Mary Jane and nine children. Stump fell in love with Balch's eldest 16 year-old daughter Anna and asked for permission to marry her. Balch refused and the couple threatened to elope. He fired Stump and vowed to kill him if they followed through with their plan.

The couple disregarded Balch's warning and a few weeks later traveled to Vancouver where they were married in November 1858. The pair honeymooned and returned to East Portland (a separate city then) where other members of the Stump family lived.

Danford Balch took the elopement news harshly, falling into deep depression, insomnia and heavy drinking. His wife's constant needling regarding his threat provoked him towards drastic action.

Mortimer Stump, his new bride and his parents had just finished buying furniture for their new house in downtown Portland. They had loaded the furniture on a wagon and boarded the Stark Street ferry that crossed the Willamette to return to their new home. Danford Balch was lingering nearby when the wagon passed him. He had a harsh exchange with the elder Stump and followed the foursome as they boarded the ferry.

He approached Mortimer and shot his son-in-law fatally twice in the face and upper chest with a shotgun. Balch was quickly apprehended and imprisoned, but escaped from the local dilapidated wooden jail before his trial.

He camped out as a fugitive on his property before being arrested six months later after refusing to pay a $1,000 bribe to the infamous town marshal James Lappeus. He was put on trial and convicted for Stump's murder. He was hung on October 17, 1859, the first recorded legal execution in Oregon Territory. His wife remained on the property and turned to ethically challenged attorney John H. Mitchell for assistance. Mitchell's lifetime of duplicity and later political intrigue was never more blatant than with his handling of the Balch family property.

He divvied up parcels to local influential individuals including Henry Pittock and ultimately defrauded the family of their land claim. When the Balch children reached the age of majority and tried to reclaim their land, Mitchell pled that the statute of limitations had expired and he was not tried.

The land was eventually given to the City of Portland and converted into Forest Park minus any credit to Danford Balch. In 1929, a stone structure was constructed to house restrooms and later a ranger station near the site of the Balch cabin. The structure is accessible by a winding descending path named the Lower Macleary Trail.

Vandalism and damage from an infamous 1962 Columbus Day storm prompted the remaining roof and fixtures to be removed. The cost of demolition was considered too expensive and the shell remains. Over time, the structure was called the *Witches Castle* due to its forlorn appearance.

The isolated location and rumors of haunting, have created a secondary purpose for the deteriorated stone structure.

Teenagers have routinely chosen the location for evening and weekend parties. The spirits claiming to have been viewed include the ghosts of Mortimer Stump and members of the Balch family. The more like *spirits* however, have more been those consumed by successive years of teenage revelers.

Witches Castle
Forest Park
Lower Macleay Trail, Portland

Portland's Once Illicit Opium Trade Arrives Full Circle

The Tuck Lung building was originally constructed in 1867 in Chinatown as a temple or *joss house*. The structure later known as the Duck Lounge and Company Building housed 31 businesses including restaurants and one of the oldest grocery stores in Portland.

Consumer opium was a visibly promoted product offered through Duck Lounge and often prompted visits into Chinatown by a diverse ethnicity and gender clientele. Young men and woman from *respectable* families made pilgrimages into the quarter to experience a sampling of the exotic and forbidden. A sinister allure surrounded candlelit basement dens where practitioners laid on their sides in bunks inhaling the addictive drug through a pipe with its fragrant, seductive and smoky fumes.

Writer Mark Twain described smoking opium *as a comfortless operation, and requires constant attention.* The objective towards inhaling a vaporized wad of opium was romantically titled *chasing the dragon.*

Opium arrived into Portland during the 1850s with Chinese immigration and soon became an accepted part of their culture. In the frontier spirit of an open society, few locals initially concerned themselves with the practice or trade. Merchants offered and advertised its mainstream availability. It was an ideal product because it was legal, restrictions were absent and there were no excise taxes imposed.

During the 1860s, law enforcement agencies began campaigns demonstrating the association between opium and criminality. The US Marshall's office plastered public notices of auction sales of opium cases seized from criminals. By the 1870s, the Victorian middle and upper class had developed a paranoia regarding the drug's abuse and its influence on their children. California banned the drug outright in 1881 and seaports began regressive taxation doubling the price.

The growing demand for opium stimulated a secondary industry. Smuggling and police confiscation spurred by raids on opium dens became commonplace. Many of the Shanghai tunnel passageways were designed to evade such raids. Portland evolved into a center for illicit West Coast distribution. Opium consumption reached its peak between 1890-1893. The Port of Portland was rumored to be supplying the entire West Coast with the supplies originating from British Columbia.

In 1893, fifteen noteworthy members of the Portland establishment including the Port's top U.S. customs officials were indicted and tried on smuggling charges. The trial lingered for several years with marginal impact. Smuggling continued on a smaller scale but demand slackened. The allure of the forbidden was darkened dramatically by the reality from viewing addicts known as *opium fiends*. Enthusiasm dampened towards the drug. When the federal government officially outlawed opium in 1909, its influence had already waned significantly. This might be considered one national *war on drugs* that actually succeeded.

The Tuck Lung building continued operational until the 1980s when the remaining retail establishments and restaurants closed. The building remained unoccupied and declined noticeably as did the surrounding neighborhood. Street drinking, public urination and individuals sleeping in doorways diminished its desirability.

Ownership of the distinctive building has changed many times since the 80s. The building design retains its distinctive hexagonal windows, red columns and tiled roof reinforcing a sense of traditional Chinese architecture. Retail and service businesses are now gradually filling tenancies on the ground floor.

The most ironic building tenant is reserved for the top floor. The former opium peddling grocery space is currently occupied by a methadone clinic.

Tuck Lung Building
140 NW Fourth Avenue, Portland

A Park Of Protest and Alternative Lifestyle Congregation

Lownsdale is one of two courthouse squares that compose the Plaza Blocks adjacent to the Mark Hatfield Federal Courthouse. The land was acquired by the city of Portland in 1869 and the north square was named after Kentucky settler Daniel H. Lownsdale who settled locally in 1845. The south square park is named after Virginia native and former Iowa territorial legislator William Williams Chapman.

The two squares were segregated figuratively and literally from the outset. Chapman Square was designed for the exclusive use of women and children and featured all female gingko trees. Lownsdale was designated a *gentlemen's gathering place*.

In the center of Lownsdale Square, a 1906 Soldiers Monument was designed by West Coast sculptor Douglas Tilden in memory of Oregonians killed in the Spanish-American War. The legacy of both squares has been oriented around protest since their inception. In 1866, locals kidnapped Chinese workers, marching them onto the grounds and demanded their jobs. The Spanish American War was actively demonstrated against and labor unions and socialists championed their causes during the early decades of the twentieth century.

It is hardly surprising that the *Occupy Portland* movement of 2011 and *Black Lives Matter* manifestations of 2020 were centered on the property.

Lownsdale Square features another slice of local history by being a cruising location for the gay population throughout the twentieth century. Portland Police vice squad members frequently entrapped sexual solicitors and predators congregating in the brick restroom. The bathroom was literally destroyed by vandals with pipe bombs in the 1960s. The facility was later restored to its original appearance.

The restroom remains the city's sole downtown available men's public restroom, but the oppressive stench discourages any potential sexual activity. The exterior and interior are layered with graffiti as the 2020 protest movement inundated any pre-existing blank space. For the desperate patrons that can brave the smell, it is an outlet that incites a quick entrance and even swifter exit.

Lownsdale Square
SW Fourth Avenue and SW Main Street, Portland

Portland's Great Fire of 1873

San Francisco, Seattle and Portland have experienced and suffered major fires in their early settlement years. Seattle's inferno leveled their business district in 1889. San Francisco's 1906 Earthquake and Fire destroyed the downtown and many of the surrounding residential areas. Portland endured two major fires in successive years. The first in December 1872 began in a Chinese laundry facility along the waterfront and destroyed several blocks in the areas of Front and SW Morrison Streets.

There was a fortunate twist to this destruction eight months later. The damage had not yet been rebuilt and acted as a buffer to a much worse calamity.

At approximately 4:20 a.m. on the morning of August 2, 1873, a fire begin at the Hurgren and Shindler Furniture store on SW First Street near SW Taylor downtown. The flames were fueled by oils and varnishes within the store and spread rapidly throughout the neighborhood. In just twenty minutes, the fire had devoured an entire block. The prevailing winds shifted the inferno in various directions creating havoc for firefighters battling the fire. Firefighters from neighboring cities arrived to assist in minimizing the spreading damage.

The fire ultimately consumed over twenty-two blocks on the west side of the Willamette River destroying hundreds of commercial, retail and residential establishments. The fire eventually burned itself out lacking additional materials to consume. There were no reported fatalities.

The cause of the fire was never determined, but speculation concentrated on anti-Chinese arsonists. Portland reportedly refused financial aid offered by San Francisco and East

Coast cities. Rebuilding was slowed by the national *Panic of 1873* and required five years to accelerate reconstruction. Seattle, by contrast, began major rebuilding the year following their fire.

Portland in 1873 had a population of approximately 15,000 inhabitants compared with over 650,000+ today making it the 25th most populated American city. The crucible of the inferno today is occupied by Portland's World Trade Center complex.

1873 Portland Fire Starting Point
World Trade Center
SW First Avenue near SW Taylor Street, Portland

A Portland Institution Surviving A Tumultuous and Temperance Past

In 1874, the downtown corner of SW First Avenue and SW Alder Street staged a literal *battle between the sexes*. The issue of contention was over booze. Passive protests began with worship services and hymnals staged on sidewalks outside of prominent North End saloons. The tenor of reaction evolved from minor irritation to outright hostility.

The male patrons of the Webfoot Saloon, strong proponents of liberally flowing drink, skirmished with the female pro-temperance activists. The fighting began with insults and obscenity exchanges but soon escalated into drawn knives and pistols.

Several of the more outspoken and militant temperance women were arrested. Decades later, the anti-drinking reformers would prevail when Oregon outlawed alcoholic beverages.

In 1879, the Bureau Saloon would open at the Webfoot's location. The name would be permanently changed upon Frank Huber's purchase of the property. Today, Huber's Restaurant promotes itself as Portland's oldest dining establishment. The site of the temperance battle and former Bureau Saloon are located below the foundations of a Bank of America Financial Center.

Huber's would change location two additional times before settling on its present site on the ground floor of the Pioneer Building. That location was opened in 1910.

The structure was originally known as the Railway Express Building and designed by architect David C. Lewis. The building is one of the oldest reinforced concrete structures downtown exhibited by its exposed gray columns. It was named after its former principal tenant, the Oregon Pioneer Savings and Loan Association. Currently, the property is a 120-room Marriott HI-LO Hotel.

Huber's Restaurant features arched stained glass, skylights, mahogany paneling and terrazzo flooring. Original fixtures include spittoons, overhead lights, fans, clocks, cash resisters and pewter wine stands. The temperance movement had absolutely no lasting impact on Huber's. The restaurant is currently stocked with an expansive wine list and full bar.

**Original Webfoot and Bureau Saloon Locations
currently B of A Financial Center, 121 SW Morrison St**

Huber's Restaurant, 411 SW Third Avenue, Portland

Liverpool Lil: Honest Larceny and Debauchery

Elizabeth *Liverpool Lil* Smith, in the grandest and most scandalous fashion of frontier Portland, operated the Senate Saloon in the North End. There was little pretense regarding the operations of her building the Norton House, constructed in 1875 featuring Italianate architecture. Downstairs was reserved for alcohol consumption and gambling. Upstairs was dedicated towards prostitution and lodgings.

Lil obtained her nickname because she was British and her predominantly sailor clientele originated from the port city of Liverpool. Her brothel became their Portland bank and port. She was reputed to be the sole individual within the North End that could be trusted with an envelop of cash. Her establishment featured an enormous safe behind the bar protecting incoming sailors and loggers from getting *rolled and robbed* by unscrupulous thieves, gamblers and whores.

Although many would ultimately blow their earnings at *Lil's* establishment, there existed an ethics to the larceny. At least they knew where their funds had evaporated.

Lil's character would never be mistaken for piety. Her reputation for lightening wallets originated from slow days when only four or five customers appeared to be patronizing her saloon. An occasional sucker would enter the bar and order a round of drinks for everyone. *Lil* would alert her girls upstairs via a hidden bell chord and all of them would flock downstairs ordering champagne on the visitor's tab. Instead of getting off cheap for his *generosity*, he would be stuck with an exorbitant bill.

Lil incurred the unrestrained wrath and condemnation of N. J. Blagen, a Danish immigrant, who constructed his distinctive four-story Blagen Block across the street from her in 1897. The building is the last remaining example of rhythmic rows, columns and arches that formerly united block fronts in downtown Portland. His architectural gem was leased to W.C. Noon for sail manufacturing employing up to eighty-three seamstresses. The view below inside the Senate Saloon proved distracting to his employees. Many were harassed by bar patrons as they daily entered the company headquarters for work. The Blagen Block today operates as a customer experience center for the San Francisco-based Airbnb online hospitality service.

Liverpool Lil was considered a shrewd businesswoman, but erred regarding the bicycle fad during the 1890s. Originally invented bicycles started as dangerous sport featuring enormous front wheels. This design flaw created significant risks when navigating downhill slopes and/or contact with unforeseen obstacles. The design also provided an unflattering view of women (not necessarily for men) who'd accidentally tangled their skirts inside the spokes.

The modified safety bicycles of the 1890s eliminated both dangers and popularity exploded nationally. *Lil* purchased a bicycle track, strategically situated a saloon in the center and promoted the venue by outfitting her employees in extravagant riding costumes with precariously slit skirts. Her tactics drew attention, but not necessarily her desired objective.

Her scandalous advertisers scared *respectable* Portland women from joining their ranks. The bike craze evaporated quickly in Portland and *Lil* was stuck with enormous underemployed inventory. Her saloon staggered into the early twentieth century but her clientele based withered.

In contemporary times, the Norton House remains vacant seeking occupancy for legitimate tenants. The building touts its former retail storefronts, offices and even employment as a basket factory. The property even promotes itself as a former *first class* lodging establishment where President Ulysses S. Grant once stayed. More appropriately, if Grant indeed lodged there, it was under *Liverpool Lil's* reign when he was known as *Soldier Ulysses S. Grant,* given his notorious and unsanitized reputation for debauchery.

Norton House
33-53 NW First Avenue, Portland

Blagen Block
30-34 NW First Avenue, Portland

A Bare *Boneyard* Alternative for the Destitute

The Oregon Steam Navigation Company's (OSN) *Boneyard* was a notorious 19th century northern Portland shipping graveyard in the Albina district along the Willamette River. Antiquated and dilapidated riverboats were parked awaiting their final demise. Most were maintained in the event replacement parts were required for still operational boats.

The chaotic and deteriorating assemblages nurtured a colony of social outcasts and recluses seeking isolation. The colony of vagrants and transients occupied some of the derelict wreckages and one known prostitute, Eliza *Boneyard Mary* Bunets offered her services for the daring and desperate. A drowning that she claimed to have potentially witnessed may have in fact been a murder that she committed. The *Boneyard* was considered a worst-case scenario destination. For some visitors, it became a final destination, particularly when their lifeless bodies floated to the surface.

Many consider homelessness to be a contemporary phenomenon, but vagrancy has existed since the creation of collective settlements. Today, the social dilemma has expanded beyond a single confined urban district or neighborhood. Downtown and North End Portland supports a subculture of residents unshielded from harsh elements and increasingly evidently housed in temporary pup tents squatting in parking lots, doorways and even on public sidewalks.

The fate of storied *Boneyard Mary* has long ago dissolved into irrelevance. Like her, many of Portland's homeless population will likely never reach an advanced age. Their streetside contemporaries will solely mourn their fated suffering and demise.

The Oregon Railway and Navigation Company in 1879 purchased the OSN stockyard. Steamboat routes were displaced by trains and then ultimately by the automobile and connecting roadways and bridges. The *Boneyard* was eventually sanitized and the space is currently utilized as a US Army Corps of Engineers Terminal. The industrial employment of the property discourages public access.

Former Boneyard Location
US Army Corps of Engineers Terminal 2
3556 NW Front Avenue, Portland

Society Hotel: Sanctuary From A Hostile Maritime Environment

In 1881, Old Town Portland was a perilous and hazardous destination for sailors navigating the local streets. Today's gritty neighborhood remains equally frightening. The Portland Seamen's Friend Society constructed a local sanctuary called the *Mariner Building* as a safe harbor and boarding house for visiting mariners intended to shield them from the prevalent alcohol, drugs, prostitution and Shanghaiing practices of local crimps. Many of the existing seamen's boardinghouses then were complicit in the kidnapping trade as a supplemental source of income.

An affiliate of the American Seamen's Friends Society based in New York, the Portland organization completed the Justus Krumbein designed three-story structure in 1882. Residents of the property were obliged to refrain from drinking and attend bible study and singing classes during their stay. In 1891, an adjoining church was constructed. The existing brick structure was elevated and a new first floor added.

The Seamen's Friends Society eventually suffered their own schism with internal squabbling and excessively incurred debt. They were forced to sell the property in 1903 to the Hip Sing Association, a Chinese based Tong association. The ground floor became a Chinese dance hall and social activity center.

A Japanese couple owned and operated the property before being interned during World War II. The building later became the Queen's Hotel, a dry goods store and an infrequent movie set. Former *gypsy royalty* were rumored to be residents following an elaborate funeral procession amidst the streets of Portland.

In 2013, four business partners acquired the building and completed an entire renovation. In the fall of 2015, the Society Hotel opened featuring an affordable 24-bed communal sleeping space, kitchenettes, lockers, lounge area and *desirable* centralized proximity to downtown Portland and the Pearl district.

Society Hotel
203 NW Third Avenue, Portland

A Revenge Murder in Portland's Historic *Court of Death*

Carrie Bradley arrived in Portland during the late 1870s in her early twenties and by 1881 was operating a small brothel amidst an established red-light district. Labeled by the *Portland Morning Oregon* as the *Court of Death*, the notorious block was framed by SW Third and SW Fourth Streets on one periphery and SW Taylor and SW Yamhill on the other. Her parlor location became known for higher end courtesans, compared with streetwalkers working the waterfront district.

Bradley developed a cozy financial relationship with Portland Chief of Police James Lappeus who overlooked flagrant activities rampant in her establishment. Professor Otto Jordan played soothing piano music as clients sipped spiked brandy. Many clients indulged in dabbing chloroform on their upper lip before retiring with their temporary dates upstairs.

Bradley's operation generally evaded scrutiny until retiree James Nelson Brown arrived in Portland, checked into the waterfront National Hotel (since demolished), patronized every visible bar and brothel and eventually visited her establishment. Brown selected fetching prostitute Dolly Adams who lightened his pocket of $6 by the time he awoke the next morning. Brown immediately filed a complaint with the district attorney's office.

District Attorney J. M. Caples was receptive to Brown's plight as he'd been assembling evidence against Bradley for months in an attempt to permanently close her establishment. Caples informed Police Chief Lappeus regarding his new star witness and ensuing plan of action. Soon Carrie Bradley was aware of the district attorney's intentions.

Bradley's plan of attack was elemental; eradicate John Nelson Brown before a public trial. For three months, Brown had prudently avoided Bradley's establishment. Pete Sullivan had been hired by Bradley to befriend Brown in order to accomplish the task by means of charm, force or drugging. On Friday evening, October 28, 1881 shortly before the trial, Pete Sullivan nonchalantly isolated Brown at Chauncey Dales's Grotto Saloon on SW Morrison Street between SW First and SW Second Avenues.

They were joined coincidentally by Carrie Bradley and Dolly Adams who liberally flirted with Brown and feigned jovial forgiveness over their past dispute. As the drinks and cheeriness flowed liberally, Bradley convinced Brown even greater pleasures awaited him at her parlor offered directly by the proprietress.

The smitten lamb followed his temptress into a liquor-induced doom. He continued to drink profusely laudanum-laced brandy and soon was unconscious. He was stripped to only his shirt, collar and tie and hauled upstairs. Bradley reportedly burned the rest of his clothing and then securely tied a handkerchief over Brown's nostrils drenched in chloroform. She left Brown prostrate overnight insuring he would properly expire. In the morning, certain that he was dead, she pummeled his face with blows accentuated by a set of procured brass knuckles. She swore a cascade of oaths against Brown and District Attorney Caples. In a reported frenzy, she vowed vengeance against anyone employed in her house that reported the death to the coroner.

Bradley attempted to bury Brown's body in the cellar. The rock and gravel base made excavation to the proper depth impossible. On Sunday evening, she and three associates rented a horse drawn carriage. The carriage was brought to the back of the house. Brown's body was situated in an upright position inside with one of Bradley's hired help sitting beside. The other two men sat outside.

The carriage was steered down Second Street to a wharf near the current Steel Bridge along the Willamette River. A one hundred pound stone was attached to Brown's neck and his heels were bound with wire. The three men rowed a boat presumably to midstream and dumped him in the river.

One months later, the corpse was sighted during low tide and retrieved by a small boat in the shallow waters near the Weidler's Steam Mill shipping docks on the west bank near the foot of NW Savier Street. Two of Bradley's prostitutes, Dolly Adams and Mollie Flippin, who'd prudently remained silent regarding the affair, visited the morgue the day after recovery and reportedly identified the body. Their sudden courage was prompted by Bradley's abrupt disappearance.

She'd foreseen the possibility that she might need a hasty escape and had prepaid Police Chief Lappeus for the option. Whether he held up his end of the bargain was debatable. She booked passage from Victoria, British Columbia to San Francisco on the steamer *Idaho*. She was arrested upon arrival and calmly but defiantly denied any knowledge regarding the murder.

Two of her accomplices were arrested in Yolo County and San Francisco, California the same day. One of the men involved in the body disposal vanished entirely. All of the arrested were indicted for murder along with Dolly Adams and Mollie Flippin.

At trial, Dolly Adams, who testified for the prosecution, recited the published narrative of events. Bradley attempted unsuccessfully to accuse Adams of the murder. Adams would only serve a brief jail term due to her cooperation and changed her name upon release. Bradley's primary accomplice, Pete Sullivan pled guilty and served four years at the Oregon State Penitentiary.

Carrie Bradley was convicted of manslaughter and sentenced to twelve years in prison. After serving five years, she was released and relocated to Mount Shasta where she opened another brothel. Her association with Sullivan remained tethered as he recruited women in San Francisco for employment in her new parlor. He was arrested for soliciting and sentenced to five years at San Quentin. Verifying she indeed possessed a vulnerable heart and possibly remorse, Bradley shot herself shortly after Sullivan's imprisonment. Police chief James Lappeus was ultimately fired the following year upon the disclosure of his arrangement with Carrie Bradley.

Today the *Court of Death* is a seven-story parking garage facility incorporated into the Pioneer Place shopping mall. The structure features ground floor retail tenants.

Former Court of Death Location (currently SmartPark Structure)
818 SW Fourth Avenue, Portland

**Drop Off Point of John Nelson Brown's Body
Steel Bridge Base, Portland**

**Location Where Brown's Body Was Discovered
Former Location of Weidler's Steam Mill
Foot of NW Savier Street, Portland**

A Solitary French Courtesan's Prolonged Cold Case Murder

Lone Fir Cemetery is Portland's oldest and ironically the community's second largest arboretum with over 700 trees. Sixteen former Portland mayors are buried amidst the 30 acres, crowned by sculptural monuments, headstones and gothic mausoleums.

Amidst over 25,000 graves, nearly 40% are unmarked commemorating forgotten lives. One elevated tombstone acknowledges a solitary 35-year-old French courtesan killed by an ax-murderer inside her working cottage on December 22, 1885. Anne Jeanne Tingry-Le-Coz's body was discovered lying face down in a three-foot-wide pool of blood. She was the victim of a gruesome slashing that local newspapers reported in explicit detail. She was reportedly clad in only her nightgown, stockings and boots. Le Coz practiced her trade under the pseudonym *Emma Merlotin*.

During this period, violence against female prostitutes accelerated resulting in numerous flagrant abuse and homicides. Police considered their protection a low priority. A prime suspect discovered near the murder scene was arrested days later. Finnish sailor William Sundstrom was detained but never charged for her murder. Sundstrom was a compelling suspect of interest because he had bloodstains on his clothing and was carrying a hatchet. No additional suspects would be arraigned making the killing one of Portland's most notorious unsolved murders.

Merlotin did not die a pauper. An intriguing twist occurred nearly a year following her death. The acting French vice council received a proof of heirship notification from her brother Joseph Le Coz. The 58-year old LeCoz worked in a tobacco factory in Morlaix, France. His pursuit of her estate required significant persistence. The proof of heirship was a voluminous document attested by six authorities including the American consul-general in Paris. At stake with his claim was a half interest in a lot and building on Front Street (near Alder), a considerable sum of money and jewelry.

Le-Coz is considered the most renowned grave in a cemetery full of anonymous phantoms. Her tomb is located in nearly the exact center of the burial park. Her former cottage location is currently situated on the periphery of the former *Court of Death* property, a downtown parking lot with retail tenants on the ground floor.

Location of Anne Jeanne Tingry-Le-Coz's Cottage
SW Third Avenue and SW Yamhill Street, Portland

Anne Jeanne Tingry-Le-Coz's Gravestone
Lone Fir Cemetery, Section 20, Lot 18, Gravesite 2S
SE 26th Avenue and Stark Street, Portland

Alice Oberle: A Celtic Cross and a Family's Shame

Centered amidst the shadowy memorials that populate Lone Fir Cemetery is an unmarked distinctive Celtic cross. Someone has purposely scratched a visible cross in the center of one side without explanation.

The memorial was originally designated for Alice Oberle, a well-known local prostitute renowned as the *Fancy Lady*. Long before the contemporary social media's obsession with self-promotion, Oberle was credited with servicing over 6,000 lovers under the tutelage of her sister Flora, coincidentally her Madame.

Alice Oberle barely reached thirty before succumbing to cirrhosis of the liver in 1884. Her legacy was acknowledged by her former clients who pooled their funds and purchased the cross memorial with a cenotaph and inscription. Flora died five years later and the sisters were buried together.

In 1911, another sister, Marie Sauvie died and her family decided to relocate the scandalous aunts' remains to Mt Calvary Cemetery in Portland. The women are buried with other members from the Sauvie family. A banal rectangular flat stone with an inscribed *R.I.P.* identifies Alice. The family had the cenotaph and inscription removed permanently from the Lone Fir memorial.

The Celtic cross remains one of the more impressive remembrances within the cemetery grounds despite the absence of remains underneath. Strollers pass regularly past the cross unaware of its significance or about the history of the woman whose prodigious sexual appetite had no peer during her era.

Alice Oberle's Celtic Cross Memorial
Lone Fir Cemetery, Block 13/Lot 17/3N
SE 26th Avenue and Stark Street, Portland

Merchants Hotel: A Storied History Reconstructed Primarily Underground

The Merchant Hotel was completed in 1884 and remains one of the most distinctive examples of Victorian Italianate architecture within Portland's Old Town district. The property was designed by Warren Heywood Williams and occupies half of a city block.

The luxury hotel required four years to build and was originally owned by brothers Louis, Adolph and Theodore Nicolai. Upon completion, it became one of Portland's first properties to feature a hydraulic elevator. In the 1890s, musician Eugene Stebinger purchased the building.

The hotel's ground floor was historically employed as a bar and billiards room and a portion of the upper rooms as a brothel. The hotel operations officially ceased in 1967. A much needed renovation and restoration followed with a ground floor tenancy by a large furniture store. Upper floors were converted into office space.

What currently distinguishes the Merchant Hotel is the Japanese Museum of Oregon on the Couch Street façade and its three prominent foodservice tenants.

Old Town Pizza is located in the original lobby where a legendary elevator was once strategically positioned. The storied elevator no longer exists but the space has evolved into a cozy booth space for visiting diners and drinkers. The apparition of a prostitute named Nina occupies the confines and imaginations of Merchant Hotel visitors.

Nina was recruited into white slavery and then into the designs of traveling missionaries attempting to eradicate vice from the neighborhood. Nina apparently cooperated but her efforts prompted a fatal push down the Merchant's elevator shaft. Her spirit has been rumored to remain in and underneath the building prompting suspicious paranormal activities.

A corner Starbucks outlet has been strategically lodged into the building complex along with the arguably most populated establishment, the Hobo restaurant. The Hobo is the origin and termination point for the fabled Shanghai Underground Tours. A streetside access trapdoor in front of the restaurant ushers patrons into the seamy world of crimpers and the neighborhood's criminal past.

The tales of legendary Joseph Bunko Kelly are spun with sincerity and accompanied by supporting props including a replica of his famed cigar store Indian. Among the reconstructed elements included in the visit are an opium den, rudimentary Chinese tin can alarm system, barroom trap door and holding prison wedged within stubborn and often unaccommodating contemporary piping, electrical wiring and city imposed structural steel supports. On a fortunate tour, you may hear Nina's curling shrieks or view her disoriented silhouette. You most certainly will hear the audible barista orders from the Starbucks above ground.

A network of intricate subterranean tunnels extends throughout the downtown. They originally connected to the Willamette River waterfront. Portions may have indeed been employed for kidnapping sailors and women into white slavery. In Chinatown, tongs (secret societies) operated opium, gambling and illicit dens. The necessity for escape passages from police raids made tunneling pragmatic.

Yet the shear number and length of the network defy easy explanation. The tunnels often served as an expedient subterranean transfer passageway for goods and individuals. Much of their actual employment has become speculation since minimal documentation was known regarding their existence for decades.

The sinister motives always generate far greater interest however.

Merchants Hotel
121 NW Second Avenue, Portland

The Legendary Exaggerations Behind Joseph *Bunko* Kelly

Portland's most notorious late nineteenth century villain arrived into the city from presumably Liverpool, Dublin and/or Connecticut, depending upon the historian. Joseph *Bunko* Kelley's most prominent character trait was his propensity towards self-promotion and exaggeration. Operating in an era absent of reliable fact checking, the chronicle of his life is left to imaginative writers.

Kelly's most quoted biographer, Stewart Holbrook embellished his tales to a generally gullible Left and East Coast press. Holbrook's versions were published during the 1930s and 40s and were frequently credited reminiscences of one Edward *Spider* Johnson, a former bartender at Erickson's legendary saloon.

As with literary spinner Mark Twain, Holbrook's distinction between fact and fiction became irrelevant. Holbrook was a credible journalist laboring for three decades with *The Oregonian* newspaper. Unlike Twain, Bunko Kelly and Holbrook remain generally forgotten except within Portland historical circles and underground tunnel tour guides. Holbrook's additional claim to fame was his reported early 1960s founding of the James G. Blaine Society, an organization whose main objective was to prevent people from moving to Oregon. The society exploited a popular statewide sentiment during the decade, particularly oriented towards Californians.

Certain factual elements of Kelley's life are documented. It is generally acknowledged that he was a crimp, a waterfront character that specialized in the trade of furnishing unwilling sailors to sea captains requiring crew members. The practice called *Shanghaiing* involved kidnapping men through trickery such as barroom trap doors, intimidation and usually violence. Shanghai, China was a common destination for ships with abducted crews earning the nefarious distinction.

The practice was necessitated by labor shortages due to the extended durations of sea voyages, low pay and abysmal shipboard conditions. English sea captains encouraged the practice and particularly escape by crew members just before the voyage's termination. They were not obliged to pay wages until their arrival at the destination port. The cost savings earned captains supplementary income.

Kelly was mentioned during early 1887 in *The Oregonian* for various legal matters. The first time was when he was sued for liable by naming a competitor as the responsible party for the suspected shanghaiing of a local printer named Fulton. The second was when he sued the captain of the ship *Africa* for refusing to pay him for a provided sailor. Kelly won the judgment. The third instance was when the sea captain of the British ship *Jupiter* sent a letter to the editor stating: *I was swindled in Portland by Bunko Kelly shipping a man on board of my ship, a perfect cripple by rheumatism. The man did no work on the ship...for the whole passage.*

Kelly promoted himself in the 1880s and 90s as the *King of the Crimps* and credited his nickname to his cunning, boldness and absence of ethics when confronted with seemingly insurmountable odds.

Two stories recounted by Holbrook magnified Kelly's ingenuity navigating a pressing deadline and desperate manpower shortage. The tales elongate the peripheries of credibility. The first anecdote involved Kelly stealing a six-foot tall carved wooden Indian stolen from Wildman's cigar shop. He wrapped the sculpture in a tarpaulin and passed it off as a sailor for fifty dollars compensation. After discovering the deception, sailors reportedly tossed the sculpture into the Colombia River. Two days later, Finnish salmon fishermen discovered the artwork ensnared in their nets near Astoria, the gateway to Oregon's Pacific Ocean access. The Indian was returned to Wildman's.

The second narrative exemplified Kelly at the peak of his prowess. In 1893, he was desperately short of manpower to fill a holiday order for the *Flying Prince*. He needed to supply twenty-four men at the compensation rate of thirty dollars per head. In some versions, the demand reached thirty-nine men. His scouring expedition throughout the quiet North End had initially left him empty of recruits. Providence or Satan provided him a solution.

Kelly noticed an open trapdoor in the sidewalk typically used as a delivery portal for businesses without alley access. Inside he found twenty-four men sprawled on the floor unconscious. Depending on the source, a percentage of them or perhaps all were dead. Reportedly, the group had attempted to burglarize the cellar of a saloon next door. A keg they discovered was filled with lethal embalming fluid instead of alcoholic spirits.

Every member drank past the point of intoxication. Kelly transported the survivors and/or corpses to the *Flying Prince* for his due commission. Once again, Astoria became the disposal destination for the cadavers. In other accounts, the ship completed its appointed itinerary stocked with the stiffs on board. The only aspect of the tale remotely credible was that kidnapped sailors were often delivered severely drugged or unconscious to inhibit an inconvenient resistance to their imposed fate.

Holbrook's fable indicated that the local Astoria press made great headway with the story. At this juncture of such an improbable story, the line separating confirmed fact from creative license deviated riotously. Researchers have been unable to track either story in Astoria or Portland newspaper archives or any documentation regarding the existence of the *Flying Prince* in the records of *Lloyds of London*, the insurance outlet for the majority of British cargo vessels.

The Bunko Kelly legend was fanned by his arrest and trial for the murder of elderly saloonkeeper G. W. Sayres, a Portland based opium smuggler for reasons historically vague. Kelly was reputed to be selling clay as fake opium to the local Chinese population. Kelly reportedly beat Sayres to death and dumped him in the Willamette River with Sayres still wearing his gold watch and carrying jewelry. Leaving valuable jewelry intact seemed an odd oversight for such a petty criminal.

Kelly proclaimed his innocence for Sayres' murder maintaining that a former employer, Larry Sullivan had framed him. Sullivan was a former boxer who realized crimping and drug smuggling were far more lucrative. An 1894 sketch of Kelly during his trial in the Portland Evening Telegram portrayed a square faced man with a wide jaw, heavy mustache and hair loss across the temples. He was also described as *squat* and *barrel chested,* but some of his closest intimates merely labeled him *common* and *cheap*.

Kelly was convicted of second-degree murder and sentenced to life in prison. The closely followed trial for a vicious murder and a memorable name elevated his status into public notoriety. A crowd of spectators reportedly arrived at the Portland railway station to glimpse the celebrity prisoner on his way to prison. Viewing the drab and diminutive Kelly instead of a thunderous goliath proved a disappointment to their expectations.

Upon his release, Kelly authored his memoir *Thirteen Years in the Oregon State Penitentiary*. Profound in deeper levels of amplification and short of supporting proof, Kelly claimed to have fought in the Civil War in the Southern Navy, a Cuban uprising and as part of a coup d'etat in Chile. His most outrageous claim is that he had been shipwrecked on an island of cannibals and obliged to survive from the flesh of his shipmates. The intent of the book was to castrate the prison conditions he'd endured and cash in on his self-perceived celebrity. His text was coarse but inventive. Kelly lacked the charisma to endear himself to an indifferent public. The book failed to sell.

His release had been accelerated by a pardon from Oregon's Governor Chamberlain in 1908 in response to clemency petitions from influential individuals. Kelly embarked on a two-year book promotional odyssey in Seattle and San Francisco that confirmed his irrelevancy. It was rumored in the *San Francisco Call* newspaper that he worked briefly for local political fixer Abe Ruef who was in the midst of his own professional fall from grace.

Crimping became illegal with the 1915 Congressional Seaman's Act. The practice became unnecessary by the advent of steam-powered ships making most unskilled labor redundant. Joseph *Bunko* Kelly evolved into a prominent and sinister face behind an evil act. His imagined role however as *King of the Crimps* was likely confined to the space separating his temples and the imagination of a tongue-in-cheek scribe.

Portland Evening Telegram's **1894 Image of Joseph Bunko Kelly**

Fasting With Fatal Consequences

In the late nineteenth century, fasting achieved a cult fascination amongst wealthy individuals seeking to purify themselves physically and morally through vows of abstinence.

In the state of Washington, self-professed Doctor Linda Hazzard established a sanitarium that was responsible for dozens of deaths through literally starving her clients. Her institution was nicknamed *Starvation Heights* due to the skeletal residents roaming the grounds. She was convicted of manslaughter for the death of one wealthy patient primarily because she absconded with the woman's assets. She was released after serving only two years at the Washington State Penitentiary and resumed her practice in the discreet foothills of the Olympic Peninsula. Her own death came in 1938 while attempting a fasting cure.

Portland had its own version of a fasting cult during the same era involving the fanatical Kate Ann Williams. It was concentrated within an enormous Victorian mansion located downtown on the corners of NW Eighteenth and Couch Streets. Former U. S. Attorney General George H. Williams, one of the primary architects of Reconstruction for the defeated Civil War Confederate states, owned the property.

Williams storied career included stints as a United States Senator, Oregon Supreme Court Chief Justice and Mayor of Portland. His eccentric wife Kate Ann initiated and became the leader and prophetess of a fasting movement. The sect originally met in the Williams' living room until Kate Ann began hearing instructions from God and reinforced membership commitments with rigorous 40-day fasts.

The consequences from such extreme behavior resulted in the suspected starvation death of some adherents and the confirmed death of 50-year old Alice Wells. Wells had undertaken a 40-day fast and launched into another one after a too short recuperation period. She died during the fifth week of her second fast.

The repercussions from Well's death triggered Kate Ann William's decent into her most extreme commitment towards purification. For the next four months she devoted herself to a diet of eating nothing but a morsel of communion bread and a sip of wine each day. The absence of tangible nourishment eventually proved fatal. In April 1894 during her extended 110-day experiment, she perished from starvation at the age of 61.

The notorious original mansion was demolished in 1916. An annex townhouse structure had been constructed in 1883 on the northwest corner of the property. It was relocated to the former mansion site in 1922 following the demolition. The structure was built as an investment and Williams never actually resided there. It became known as *The Lawn* and during the 1960s featured 32 budget apartments sharing two toilets and a single bathtub. The site proved ideal for financially challenged student, artist and musician renters. The complex was subsequently reincarnated, subdivided and rechristened as the George H. Williams Townhouses.

TWISTED TOUR GUIDES.com

**George H. Williams Townhouses
133 NW Eighteenth Avenue, Portland**

If Walls Could Speak: A Trio of Century Old Portland Landmarks

History is often documented and displayed within the archives of museums, academic institutions and ornate but stagnant memorials littering cities globally. History however is often fermented within the intimate confines of drinking and eating establishments, where alcoholic libations liberate thought processes and hatched plots that vary from the improbable to innovative.

Three Portland establishments have weathered over a century each of changes including Prohibition, two World Wars and the shifting tides of innovation, real estate values, fashion and political regimes. All three feature tunneling underneath that may have been employed for alleged Shanghaiing sailors, opium or gambling dens and/or linkage to a unique early history subterranean transport passage.

Kelly's Olympian was founded in 1902 and has become most renowned for the current owner's airborne displayed motorcycle collection. An expansive basement reveals traces of a Prohibition-era speakeasy. The strangest reported discovery on the bar level is a rudimentary flush system and former urine trough carved into the foot of the bar. Its rumored intent was to allow male patrons to pee into the trough without displacing their location. This convenience guaranteed an unimpeded flow of drink orders.

The White Eagle was founded in 1905 and operated initially as a bar for Polish immigrant industrial workers. The establishment was also lowlighted by a basement and an eleven room upper level brothel. Located near the Fremont Bridge, the exposed brick walls, dark wood back bar and mosaic-tiled flooring accommodate contemporary live musicians and haunting restless spirits.

The ghostly apparitions identified have included a former prostitute named Rose, a pre-Prohibition bartender named Sam and the various violent brawlers that earned the saloon the nickname *bucket of blood*.

The youngest of the building trio is known for its distinctive menu rather than beverage legacy.

Meinert Wachsmuth stowed away on an ocean-going vessel from Denmark at the age of 14 in 1842. He sailed the world and crossed the Cape Horn seven times before the 1865 shipwreck of his schooner *Annie Doyle* terminated his maritime career at Yaquina Bay, Oregon. In the aftermath, he married, fathered three sons and relocated to San Francisco in 1881 to establish a family seafood business.

He retired in 1903 selling his entire holdings. The three Wachsmuth Brothers relocated to Portland. Youngest brother, Louis worked tirelessly as an oyster shucker, cook and deliveryman of seafood between SW Second and SW Third Avenues on Ankeny Street. He opened a wholesale and retail seafood outlet called *Oregon Oyster*, specializing in oyster cocktails.

Prohibition proved advantageous for Louis Wachsmuth as he acquired the food bar located at the popular Merchant's Saloon. His food service space expanded proportionately with his growing client base. Additional serving rooms were added.

With his marriage in 1908 and expansion of his own family, Louis began ambitious plans integrating his sons into the business. His second eldest son Dan died at 27 in 1938 from complications of influenza. His name was added to the company identity as a memorial. Today the business, Dan and Louis Oyster Bar remains firmly family operated. Neither scandal nor infamy has ever tainted their reputation. This evasion appears almost miraculous considering the characters and lingering stench of vice historically permeating the surrounding neighborhood.

Kelly's Olympian Bar, 426 SW Washington Street

White Eagle Saloon, 836 North Russell Street

**Dan and Louis Oyster Bar
208 SW Ankeny Street, Portland**

Kell's Famous First Alert Phantom

Kell's Irish Restaurant and Pub features a Cigar Room basement that taps into the Shanghai tunneling network commonly woven into North End folklore. Ghost and apparition sightings within the basement are not particularly novel or even a piano known to pound melodies without a visible pianist. Paranormal activity seems almost commonplace within a district where the phantoms of early Portland co-exist with the destitute temporary residents.

Haunting may easily be dismissed as fanciful imagination, but Kell's features one specific ghost with a historical lineage. He is unlike any other local phantom.

Portland Fire Chief David Campbell originally arrived in the city in 1878 and soon afterwards became a member of the volunteer fire department. In 1883 when Portland became a paid fire bureau, he was too young to be hired. Two years later he would be employed and by 1892 became Foreman of Engine Company #1. In 1895, Campbell was appointed Fire Chief by the mayor, but after fifteen months was replaced by his successor. He was reinstalled by Mayor Mason in 1898 and assumed the position until his tragic demise.

Campbell was instrumental in modernizing Portland's fire brigade by upgrading professional training and acquiring cutting edge equipment. In 1906, Portland's first fireboat was operating. Cisterns, hydrants and the central alarm system were upgraded under his watch. His proactive advocacy led to the Fire Department's transition from horse-drawn to motorized fire apparatus.

On June 26, 1911, an oil pump at the Union Oil distributing

plant located on the corner of SW Salmon and Water Streets (currently Pacific Coast Highway 99W) ignited gas accumulated in its motor pit. Ironically the site was near where the famous 1873 Portland Fire started. As the fire raged, Campbell determined the only hope for control could come from an interior attack. He borrowed a turnout coat from one of his men and disappeared into the building.

At 8:39 a.m. a rumble from the basement detonated sending bodies hurtling across the street. Tank heads flew two hundred feet in the air, the building's north wall crumpled into the street and the roof collapsed. Campbell was last viewed silhouetted against the flames, holding up his arms to brace against the falling roof.

It seems unimaginable today that the head of a municipal fire department would charge into a burning building. His funeral procession drew over 150,000 mourners in downtown. When David Campbell is viewed in the basement of Kell's, he is customarily dressed in full firefighter gear with the borrowed coat.

Kell's Irish Pub, 112 SW Second Avenue

The Open Door and Great Vice Crusade of 1896

One of the greatest reformation scams perpetuated in Portland during 1896 was a movement to construct a home *for wayward girls and fallen women.* Local churches and reformers operating in conjunction with law enforcement agencies spearheaded the movement. Police were reluctantly assigned to raid and eradicate known houses of prostitution.

The logic behind the plan was to create a refuge for reformed prostitutes where they would no longer be obliged to sell their *virtue* as their sole means of livelihood. The religious community, retail business donors and committee organizers upheld their end by delivering a North End location called the *Open Door* on NW Fifth Avenue near the intersection of Burnside Street. The building was suitably furnished and prepared for boarders under the scrupulous house watch of matron Mrs. Lucy Morgan.

Law enforcement appeared to be assuming their responsibility by arresting acknowledged Madames and prostitutes from known establishments. All were booked and released immediately after posting $100 bail. Each returned back to their establishments to await a trial date. Almost without exception, each resumed their trade immediately. A similar movement targeted gambling houses, particularly in Chinatown, amidst this immorality roundup.

At trial, if an accused perpetrator pled innocent, they were found *not guilty* for lack of proof and evidence supporting a conviction. *Guilt by reputation* proved unconstitutional. Many of the brothel's client rosters were composed of the most prominent male leaders of Portland. There was no concerted effort or concern about proving any of the allegations or eliminating these profitable institutions of vice. Only someone religiously guilt-ridden or an imbecile would opt to plead *guilty*.

The superficiality behind the law enforcement campaign was outlined in a scathing local newspaper editorial. The track record of arrests and acquittals were compared. They were equal. The same coincidence occurred with gambling arrests. The costs for arrests, trials and convictions were itemized in the editorial. It became clear that even without convictions, the district attorney, police justices and constables made healthy stipends from each case. The sham moral crusade had simply diverted taxpayer monies into the pockets of highly placed officials with no noticeable adverse impact on local gambling or prostitution.

The *Open Door* housing project flourished with applicants and tenants during the spring until the beginning of July. Then logging camps began shutting down for their midsummer break. Single men with money to incinerate and sexual scratches to itch deluged the North End. The ranks of the *Open Door* began thinning rapidly. Reality finally dawned upon the organizers. By Independence Day, house matron Morgan was alone in the accommodation. Her tenants had used the lodgings to survive the brutal spring and early summer when business was scarce. With their customer's return, opportunity and cash became plentiful once again. By the end of the summer, the *Open Door* was shuttered.

A similarly monikered *The Door* ironically would surface a half-century later in a slightly modified context. *Oregon Journal* reporter Rolla J. *Bud* Crick began a series of articles attempting to expose illicit houses of prostitution and an *abortion racket* within Portland. His larger objective may have been to expose civic corruption, police payoffs and the infiltration of organized crime into city government.

One of his contacts was a forty-four year old Madame named Goldie Lewis who complained about police harassment with her basement brothel called *The Door*. Between 1949-1954, Lewis was arrested at least nine times on morals charges of *bringing two together for immoral purposes*. She confirmed that she habitually paid off the police force, but when she didn't, *patrol cars park in front of her place* so that she would have to temporarily close her operations. The Portland police vice squad developed a notorious reputation for accepting bribes on vice related activity. Apparently this tradition had a very extended legacy.

**Open Door Building
9 NW Fifth Street, Portland**

The Door, 3237 NE Rodney Street, Portland

A Whiff of Scandal Accompanying Fine Downtown Dining

Theodore Berthus Kruse settled in Portland in 1897 following an adventurous life as a sailor from his native Germany. A shipwreck on the coast of Alaska prompted him to remain in the United States and become a citizen in 1893.

Upon his arrival in Portland, he established himself in the restaurant and catering trade. In December 1906, he purchased the elegant Louvre restaurant from Fritz Strobel inside the Belvedere Hotel. Kruse designed the interior for the city's avant-garde, decorating with nude sculptures and paintings.

The café was a known meeting place for some of the defendants in the gay vice scandal of 1912. Despite his own marriage, Kruse sexual orientation was the subject of speculation. He was rumored to trawl Seattle regularly in the company of young men *seeking new singers* for his club. He disappeared mysteriously for several weeks in 1911 without explanation. Upon his return, he claimed that he had been in Germany visiting his father. His wife divorced him discreetly shortly afterwards.

His *Bohemian* atmosphere created legal difficulties for its reported *immoral* setting and numerous liquor law violations. The café had a separate men's dining room featuring palm trees and mirror-lined walls not found in his mixed gender dining room.

The Louvre lasted until 1913, a year after its public association with the vice scandal. Kruse opened the Rainbow Grill in the Morgan Building in 1915. The name originated because its design with prisms set throughout the interior spread arrays of color. The Rainbow also featured a separate grill exclusively for men. The restaurant shuttered after only a few months of operation.

Kruse relocated to California and then later retired in Gearhart, Oregon where he died at the age of 77 in November 1941. The Belvedere Hotel was demolished in the late 1940s and the sole remnant remaining from the cafe was a large nude painting that hung above the bar of Jake's Famous Crawfish restaurant for many years. The painting no longer remains for public viewing. The Hotel Belvedere's site was replaced by a multi-level parking structure constructed in 1963.

**Former Site of Louvre Café
Tucked Between the Belvedere and Washington
Building Blocks, Belvedere Hotel, NE Corner of Fourth
and Alder, Portland**

Erickson's Saloon: Sanctuary and Exploitation Under A Singular Giant Umbrella

If a single establishment epitomized the frontier bedlam and bawdiness of Old Town Portland, Gus Erickson's monumental drinking establishment qualifies. Erickson's Saloon began in the early1880s following his immigration from Helsinki. His business offered the era's definition of *full* service.

The facility featured poker, faro, craps, roulette, pool tables, a barbershop and even an ice cream parlor. Furnished rooms and smaller prostitution cribs satisfied his client's baser urges. His downstairs complimentary buffet called *the dainty lunch* was stocked with voluptuous Scandinavian dining selections. Erickson singlehandedly eliminated the threat of hunger for laborers and the indigents living on the North End. Nicknamed *Whitechapel*, the district shared the identical name as the infamous London neighborhood where Jack The Ripper preyed upon his female victims.

Erickson comprehended what Las Vegas casinos and contemporary high technology campuses have employed decades later...keep your client base/employees stationary. Erickson offered everything conceivable to keep his male customers within his business confines. They rewarded him by spending what money they possessed.

His saloon stretched an entire city block with entrances on four sides. His mahogany bar could service in excess of three hundred drinkers. The bar ran the length of the block-long barroom from one side to the other and then back again. It was estimated to measure 684 feet if one included connecting bars. Erickson employed sixty bartenders operating in two shifts of at least thirty.

His establishment featured ornate nude paintings, statuary and silver mirrors creating an upscale appearance. This ambiance pleasured railroad workers, gold miners, loggers, fishermen, and even the criminal and unemployed class grinding away daily amidst a grim existence, Erickson's Saloon represented a simulated resort setting. The property was considered an imperative stop for visitors arriving in Portland. The interior was overflowing with boisterous conversations, laughter and music from an extravagant $5,000 pipe organ.

Erickson's success bred extensive imitators and competitors located within the neighborhood. Former associates and employees initiated many of these establishments. Erickson's however maintained the distinctive name.

Gus Erickson's fortune began to languish in 1912 when a fire gutted a portion of the premises. The structure was rebuilt in opulence, but the consequences from Oregon's 1916 Prohibition Act sealed the establishment's fate. Erickson's business floundered as a *dry saloon* offering near-beer and soda fountain drinks. Erickson would sell his interest in the property to competitor Fred Fritz who would maintain the distinctive name.

Ultimately the crowds thinned, the pipe organ was dismantled, paintings sold and the main room sectioned off until the bar comprised only a tenth of the entire square footage. The building hosted an advertising museum and later a strip joint. Erickson passed away in 1925 four years after Fritz. His obituary lauded his establishment where *the down and out found refuge*.

As Portland's North End deteriorated following World War II, the Erickson building became an inexpensive flophouse catering primarily to an impoverished population. On the evening of July 7, 1975, a 57-year-old vagrant named Roy Jennings Beard would set an arson fire on the second floor.

The fire charred the majority of the 100-room hotel's hallways and doors. Twelve people perished and 22 other men were injured in the fire. The majority of deaths were individuals who had collapsed from asphyxiation in the hallways attempting to flee the inferno. Beard never faced trial for the fire and was institutionalized as mentally incompetent at Oregon State Hospital. He disappeared from public scrutiny and presumably died at the institution.

The Erickson Saloon building today combined with the adjacent Fritz Hotel offers sixty-two low-income and market valued apartment units. In 2015, the structure was officially acknowledged as an *extraordinary* Oregon historical preservation project. The North End district remains one of Portland's slowest evolving neighborhoods, plagued by a chronic homeless population, vacant commercial spaces and a reputation for concentrated criminal activity.

Erickson's *complex capitalism* of entertainment refuge and sex exploitation will not and cannot legally be replicated today. The *free lunch* of yesteryear will also never return either.

Erickson's Saloon Building, 219 NW Second Avenue

Fritz and Erickson: A Legacy Of Two Surnames

The legacies of the surnames Erickson and Fritz seemed intertwined in turn of the twentieth century Portland history. They would later conjoined into a twenty-first century reincarnation of their former saloon establishments.

Hugo Fritz was a manager and bartender at Erickson's iconic saloon following his arrival from San Francisco in 1905. In 1906, Gus Erickson reportedly transferred the saloon license for unspecified reasons to him operating the establishment under the legal title of the Hugo Fritz Company. Fritz died in April 1908 at the age of 49.

Another Frtiz, Fred Jr. (apparently no relation) operated a saloon and theatre across the street from Erickson's on West Burnside. He would eventually acquired Erickson's saloon. In 1912, he opened the Fritz Hotel directly behind the Erickson building.

The entire neighborhood proliferated with saloons, gambling parlors, and brothels elevating Fred Fritz, Jr. into prominence as a vice lord. Wisely Fritz preserved the Erickson name and promoted his distinctive legacy. He oversaw both operations until his death at 58 in October 1921. His son, Fred A. and wife, Clara would sustain the two Portland institutions for nearly three decades afterwards. She died in 1955 and he in 1989 at the age of 94.

Aside from entertainment outlets, Fritz prudently diversified his investment base. He constructed the Villa St. Clara (named after his wife) and the Panama Building. Real estate became his secure foundation and he compounded his portfolio by acquiring numerous downtown lots and farm properties in outlying counties.

Portland's Old Town district deteriorated following World War II and the neighborhood became a magnet for an indigent street population and crime.

In 2015, the former Erickson and Fritz Saloon buildings were joined in a year-long project funded by the Portland Housing Bureau using Federal Low-Income Housing tax credits and Historic Tax credits.

During the reconstruction, salvaged materials were utilized. The original brick walls, wood staircases and railings were incorporated along with exposed charred structural beams that survived a 1975 fire. Affordable housing remains a local challenge. The Fritz and Erickson buildings with their market-rate and subsidized rents offer a welcomed alternative to a chronic housing shortage plaguing the North End.

Fritz Hotel
10 NW Third Avenue, Portland

Fritz Saloon and Theatre, 214 West Burnside

**Villa St. Clara (currently the Gentry Apartments)
909 SW Twelfth Avenue**

**Panama Building (currently the Willamette Building)
251 SW Alder Street, Portland**

Early Twentieth Century Melodrama and Making A Stand Against Homewreckers

Charles Reynolds arrived in Portland in 1902 with his much younger wife Lulu and two teenage children from a prior marriage. Lulu was raised in Salt Lake City and the couple had married in Pueblo, Colorado. Reynolds boasted proudly that he had served in the U.S. Cavalry under General George Armstrong Custer, an unproven assertion.

The family relocated from Milton-Freewater near Walla Walla where they had operated a hotel. Once established in Portland, they became part owners of a bathhouse with Mrs. M.H. McMahon and resided in a spacious home approximately fifteen blocks uptown that Lulu managed as a boardinghouse.

During their previous residence, Lulu had cultivated a passion for musical composition and a mentor by the name of George Herbert Hibbins. He billed himself publicly as *Professor Herbert*. Hibbins was familiar with Portland having been an orchestra leader in two local institutions, Laverne's Outdoor Theatre and the Star Theatre. Upon her relocation to Portland, the pair began a written correspondence that ultimately escalated into tragedy.

Hibbins' writings evolved from platonic into passion and soon he was constructing their idyllic dream castle in the air. The greatest obstacle was both were married. His initial step involved purchasing a small farm near San Diego. He was confident that pleading his case in person with Lulu would convince her in the sincerity of his plan. In his plan, both would divorce their spouses and initiate a fresh beginning of marital bliss far from the maddening crowd and conventionality.

Lulu's reaction to his strategy appeared accommodating. She arranged for his discreet lodgings in a nearby building. The couple met regularly while Charles was tending the bathhouse. Hibbins' apparently visited the Reynolds' residence periodically under the pretense of seeing one of their tenants. Charles Reynolds' children informed their father about a strange visitor embracing their stepmother with her returning the intimacy. How far their passion was consummated remained unrecorded.

Eventually Charles Reynolds became aware of his wife's duplicity. The baffled cuckold was stunned when Lulu asked him for a divorce. Using his previously honed scouting instincts, he invited her to the local Council Crest Amusement Park for a day of stilted fun but more pointedly, interrogation.

The single element the Reynolds couple's drama lacked was subtlety. Lulu had lied regarding the source of her letters, a photograph of Professor Herbert she had brazenly displayed on her piano and an extravagant promissory ring she wore gifted to her by Hibbins.

The entire farce seemed clearly destined for calamity. On Wednesday afternoon, June 20, 1907, Charles telephoned Lulu requesting her to come over to the bathhouse. She refused offering an unconvincing excuse. In some accounts, she initiated the phone call to Charles canceling their intended lunch. Lulu and Hibbins were instead seated in her parlor preparing to saunter around the neighborhood together.

Charles might have opted to discount her refusal for innumerable reasons, but when he heard a man's voice in the background saying: *Don't talk to him any more, sweetheart*, he didn't hesitate to respond. Even the densest of intellects can discern flagrant deception. He abruptly hurried to their residence armed with a loaded .38 caliber revolver.

Hibbins and Lulu sensed no alarm. They leisurely prepared for their promenade.

Hibbins had stated previously that he wanted to discuss Lulu's future with Charles in the hopes of negotiating a rational arrangement for all parties. Hibbins underestimated Reynolds' grasp of *irreconcilable differences* and his desperation towards preserving his marriage no matter how fractured. Reynolds was a creature of impulse and action, not words.

Hibbins was probably unaware that Reynolds had heard his voice over the telephone receiver. He clearly had no idea how swift a jealous and furious husband could navigate fifteen city blocks.

As he and Lulu began to step outside, Charles Reynolds clipped any perceived discussion with: *I'm onto you.* He fired three shots all striking his target. Hibbins staggered down the street and into a drugstore where he was put to bed and vainly attended to. In some reports he lingered for a few days before expiring at the Good Samaritan Hospital. One of the bullets had passed through his intestines. In other more dramatic accounts, he died of sepsis by that same late evening at 1 a.m.

When police originally arrived, they arrested Reynolds who displayed no remorse. When questioned regarding the sequence of events, Lulu whispered between tears that her relationship with Hibbins was innocent and that her husband's irrational jealousy provoked the attack. Hibbins, now the victim of potential insincerity apparently concurred upon his dying breaths.

Charles Reynolds' fate seemed damned by her seemingly sincere tale of misunderstanding. Lulu's passion however ultimately supplanted any calm or rational strategy.

Summoned to the coroner's office to identify the corpse, Lulu performed an imaginable act. She threw herself on Hibbins' lifeless body and kissed his frigid lips passionately. She confessed in explicit detail their forbidden love leading up to the shooting. She confirmed that Hibbins had lied with his last breath to shield her name.

The trial followed a more banal chronology. Charles Reynolds' defense did not deny the shooting but based it as *justifiable* against an immoral intruder sullying their sacred marriage. They based his justification on a currently en vogue *Unwritten Law* that enabled a husband to protect his possessions and family from potentially debauched intrusions. Lulu was the presumed possession. Lulu steadfastly maintained in soft tones that she had never disgraced her husband. She draped herself in a heavy veil sobbing relentlessly during the proceedings conspicuously distant from her husband and stepchildren. The trial essentially vilified Hibbins. Evidence submitted portrayed him as a callous womanizer and homewrecker.

The all male jury acquitted Reynolds in thirty minutes. His case briefly became a precedent decision. Several subsequent murder cases would follow a similar pattern. A deceived husband would conveniently slay his wife's lover under the guise of protecting their secure homestead.

Charles Reynolds publicly offered Lulu the opportunity to return back to their marriage. There is no record as to whether she accepted his offer. Her musical aspirations had ended upon the death of her mentor. Juries for killing a suspected adulterer no longer legally exonerate husbands.

The Reynolds' boardinghouse located on the corner of SW Fourteenth Avenue and SW Morrison Streets was razed and replaced by the Tiffany Center in 1928. The replacement landmark was originally known as the *Neighbors of Woodcaft Building* and served as the fraternal organization's insurance operation. The massive architectural gem features large arched openings with carved gargoyle stone elements. Wood paneling, high ceilings, polished detailing, a crystal chandelier and ornate windows create a distinctive interior art deco styling. The building was renamed the *Tiffany Center* in 1993 following the purchase by a new owner who named it after his daughter. It is currently operated as a commercial event venue featuring music and theatre within two spacious ballrooms.

Reynolds' Natatorium Baths were located on the corner of SW Second Avenue and SW Washington Street within the still standing Italianate styled Waldo Block Building originally constructed in 1886. The structure housed a bank on the bottom floor and hotel accommodations with the baths on the two upper floors. Underground tunnels formerly connected the building to the waterfront, but have subsequently been blocked off for safety reasons. The building served as a Chinese boarding house during the 1920s-40s and was reputed to be a gambling and opium den. Today, the ground floor hosts the Mama Mia Trattoria restaurant.

**Site of the Reynolds' Boardinghouse (Tiffany Center)
1410 SW Morrison, Portland**

**Former Natatorium Baths (Waldo Block Building)
201-215 SW Second Avenue, Portland**

Edgefield: From Extreme Poverty To Recreational Hospitality

Poverty and homelessness were perceived differently during the early twentieth century. The designation of being labeled *poor* was degrading, but in the majority of cases, merely a temporary setback. While impoverished urban living conditions then were often characterized by squalor and poor hygiene, those enduring extreme financial hardship had an alternative through rural agricultural employment. The Edgefield Poor Farm, addressing this condition, opened in 1911 servicing Multnomah County.

Inhabitants who'd lost their jobs would relocate there and earn lodging and meals in exchange for manual labor. The working requirement was strictly enforced under the supervision of church officials. The farm produced wheat, corn and kept livestock, essential in sustaining the population. At the peak of operations, over 700 people inhabited the 350-acre property.

For many, the stay was simply temporary until they were ready to relocate and pursue active employment. For others, their stay extended until their death. As remaining residents aged and became too infirmed to work, the focus of the operation shifted. The property transitioned into a nursing home following the economic boom of post-World War II.

By the 1960s, both the name and spotlight had been altered. The newly named Edgefield Manor ceased agriculture and became primarily a nursing home and institution for mentally ill children. By 1982, the estate was abandoned and the patients were relocated to other institutions. The vacant buildings fell into disrepair. In the early 1990s, the McMenamins brothers purchased the land and buildings from the county. They restored the property into a complex including a hotel, restaurant, vineyard, movie theatre, golf course and concert venue.

Of the thousands that have passed through the property's portals, certain obstinate spirits have opted to remain. Room 215 has become particularly popular due to a passed on narrative involving animal bones once being arranged in the shape of a large pentagram. Stories of women and children haunting the property are commonplace. Spirit-cleaning rituals employed periodically have loosened legends and sightings into the extremities of paranormal imagination.

McMenamins Edgefield
2126 SW Halsey Street, Troutdale

Mysterious Billy Smith: Portland's Most Illustrious Dirty-Fighter

Portland's brush with boxing fame came packaged in the form of Canadian born *Mysteriously Billy* Amos Smith known as possibly the *dirtiest* prizefighter in the history of the ring. Disqualified professionally an inconceivable thirteen times (many in title fights), Smith claimed the world welterweight championship in 1898. He completed his dubious career with a record of 34 wins, 25 losses, 27 draws and 5 no contests. Considering thirteen of his losses were disqualifications, his record seems less mediocre.

Turn of the twentieth century boxing might better mirror today's Mixed Martial Arts brawling except that the number of rounds then seemingly had no end. The audience sometimes interfered with the proceedings. Smith was considered a sound technical boxer, but he sullied his talent with a blatant disregard for the rules. Among his favorite tactics included elbowing, headbutting, kneeing, rabbit punching, low blows, thumbing, wrestling, hitting off the break and biting.

He began his career during the gloved era of the 1880s and reached the pinnacle of his success with the 1898 title. He lost the crown on his second defense two years later, naturally by disqualification. He staged a comeback in 1910 at the age of 39, winning a ten round bout in Oregon before losing the next year by disqualification (surprise).

On December 17, 1911, Smith was shot three times by Captain A. B. Loomis of the river steamer *We Own*. Loomis and Smith had been quarreling for four months following Loomis' marriage to Smith's ex-wife. Smith had approached her while she was walking down SW Third Avenue and West Burnside Street. They spoke briefly when

Loomis appeared suddenly firing in Smith's direction. Smith fell to the sidewalk before he could draw his own gun. Loomis struck him twice more with bullets in the abdomen. Smith's eventual return volleys veered wildly. Loomis escaped before being apprehended, but his wife was detained. Many newspapers around the country indicated that Smith had died from the shooting or would be unable to survive the night in the hospital.

He miraculously did survive his wounds.

At the time, Smith had already shuttered his Atlantic Saloon two blocks west of the site of the shooting. The saloon had been razed on the building location of the future Multnomah Hotel (now Embassy Suites) that opened the following year. Smith also operated a seamen's boarding house in Albina on the east side of the Willamette River near the grain docks. Partnering with Jim and Harry White, the operation became notorious for its more lucrative enterprise of crimping. Smith made numerous influential local enemies including competitor Larry Sullivan, a former boxer. He also incurred numerous legal scrapes including brawling with customers, gambling, bootlegging and tax evasion.

At 44, he staged his final comeback losing in the sixth round to a heavyweight named Jack Root. His son Billy, Jr fought out of Portland as *Soldier Kid Barde* between 1922-1925 and compiled a marginal professional record like his father of 9 wins, 10 losses and 4 draws.

Mysterious Billy eventually mellowed with age and expanding girth. He named his Albina based tavern *The Champion's Rest*, the identical moniker as legendary boxer John L. Sullivan christened his Boston tavern. Smith passed away on October 18, 1937 at 65. He was buried in a pioneer cemetery in an unmarked grave in lower southeastern Portland. The new owners of his Albina tavern promoted his former bar as the *Mysterious Billy Smith's Tavern* for many years following his demise. The structure located near the Broadway Bridge was demolished and replaced by the Portland Public Schools administration building.

Dante's performance club occupies Smith's former shooting site. The venue is noteworthy for its entertainment acts, but more so for the 2003 painted mural on the rear of the building promoting KEEP PORTLAND WEIRD. The slogan was copied from an identical campaign and sign originated by Austin, Texas in 2000.

**Mysterious Billy Smith Shooting Site
(currently) Dante's
350 West Burnside Street, Portland**

Keeping Portland Weird But Not Necessarily Original Mural
350 West Burnside Street, Portland

Former Champion's Rest Tavern
(currently) Multnomah County Blanchard Fleet Shop Building
301 N Dixon Street, Portland

The Unsuccessful Sexual Scandal Set-Up of Mayor Harry Lane

Two-term Portland mayor Harry Lane was perhaps one of the most idealistic and socially reformist oriented politicians in Oregon. Born in Corvallis, his father was a successful prospector during the California Gold Rush who returned to Oregon to invest his mining proceeds in the construction of a lumber mill. Lane earned his medical degree from Willamette University in Salem. He opened his medical practice in Portland where he became known as a *poor people's doctor*, often treating individuals on a pro bono basis. As his wife summarized, *he was better at making friends than making money.*

His first political experience was disillusioning. In 1887, he was selected by Oregon's Governor Sylvester Pennoyer to become the superintendent of the Oregon State Insane Asylum (today's Oregon State Hospital). He aggressively investigated charges of corruption. The corresponding political pressure from his efforts forced him to resign four years later at the urging of the governor.

Returning to his private Portland practice for the next decade, he ran for the non-partisan position of mayor in 1905. He won and would eventually served successive two-year terms.

On September 26, 1907, a local Labor party rival, E. S. Radding, conspired with 20-year-old Belle Waymire to entrap Lane in a political scandal with potential blackmail implications. There were two versions to the story. In her account, she met with him in his private office in the Hamilton Building seeking his assistance in recovering her child from the custody of her estranged husband's parents.

Without provocation, he attacked and attempted to rape her without her consent.

In court documents, the entire affair was documented differently as a set-up between Radding and Waymire designed to destroy Lane's reputation. In the legally recorded account, Waymire *set upon him*. She *grasp and held his person* and then *tore and disheveled his clothing*. She sought *to indecently expose his person*. The sole unclear issue was precisely which party was left in the most compromised position.

Where the two accounts did agree was that Radding shattered the door to Lane's office attracting attention to a group of nearby citizens. He claimed his actions were justified by hearing a woman's scream while Lane insisted the screams were part of the strategy to frame him.

The local newspapers followed the unfolding case intimately consistently backing Lane's version of events. A grand jury indicted Waymire and Radding on charges of *committing an act that outrages public decency and is injurious to public morals*. The pair pled *not guilty*, but a jury required only an hour to return a *guilty* verdict. The case reached the Oregon Supreme Court, which upheld the convictions.

Lane's tenure as mayor was generally considered ineffective as his social reform agenda contrasted markedly with local business interests. In 1905, the Lewis and Clark Centennial Exposition exposed Portland to a much wider national audience. Lane advocated a *permanent rose carnival* afterwards. He is considered the *Father of the Portland Rose Festival* that has continued annually. He was known for his advocacy of Native American and Women's rights and while in office swore in Portland's first female police officer Lola Baldwin (the second in the United States).

In 1912, he emerged victorious from a cluttered roster of candidates to earn a U.S. Senate seat representing the Democratic Party. His entire campaign budget amounted to $75 plus travel expenses. As a senator, many of his outspoken advocacy positions were farsighted but unpopular during the era. He challenged segregationalists, corporate monopolies, anti-environmentalist policies, private ownership of utility services and America's entry into World War I.

The furor over intense public and local criticism overwhelmed Lane, who had chronically suffered from ill health. He collapsed and died in route to Portland on May 23, 1917 seeking a recuperative break. Idealists such as Harry Lane historically have not flourished amidst the grime of politics.

A curious reality regarding Lane and his integrity was that the sexual impropriety charge seemed improbable. The resulting dismissal revealed the public's respect towards his uprightness. Would that same certainty exist today regarding the character of most contemporary public officials?

Hamilton Building
529 SW Third Avenue, Portland

Dr. Marie Equi: A Complicated Heroine Viewed Through Many Prisms

Dr. Marie Equi lived a life of conviction and compassion that her peers, comrades and even enemies could acknowledge. Her legacy was not entirely crystalline. Admired icons are not historically labeled as *blackmailers* and this taint blemished an otherwise exemplary life lived on her terms. She was a voice of conscience honed by action and principle. She suffered dearly for these principles.

Born in 1872 and raised in New Bedford, Massachusetts, she was the fifth child and fifth daughter in a large working class family. She quit high school after a single year and supported herself by working in a local textile mill. Ill-fitted for conservative New England and fearlessly unconventional, she migrated to an Oregon homestead in 1892, residing with a high school girlfriend, Bessie Holcomb.

From an early age, she expressed no interest in a heterosexual relationship or marriage. Throughout her lifetime, she never compromised on her sexual preferences or her conviction that women be treated on equal terms as men. She never advocated the women's separatist movement and worked comfortably with men on both a professional and political basis. Her publicly avowed relationships with women established her defiantly as one of the West Coast's first publicly recognized lesbians.

In 1897, Equi and Holcomb lived together on over 100 acres outside the settlement of The Dalles. Holcomb taught at the Wasco Independent Academy for their exclusive source of income. On July 21, 1893. School superintendent and local real estate developer, Reverend Orson D. Taylor attempted to renege on paying Holcomb her entire teaching salary. Frustrated by his duplicity, Equi stalked the cowering Taylor with a whip before a gathering crowd of onlookers. When he attempted to flee, she horsewhipped him to the delight of the audience.

She was arrested, but members of the community reportedly posted her bail in defiance to the unpopular Taylor. Whether Holcomb was ever properly compensated was never recorded, but reportedly the town held a raffle for the whip and gave the proceeds to both women.

Afterwards the couple relocated to San Francisco where Marie Equi began her medical studies requiring two years. She relocated to Portland without Holcomb and completed her studies at the University of Oregon Medical School in 1903.

Equi became one of the first sixty women to become a physician in Oregon. She established a Portland medical practice emphasizing women and children's health issues. She also treated men. She was lauded for her patient care to individuals from all social classes and income levels. She typically charged her wealthier patients more to compensate for the expenses incurred in treating poorer patients.

In 1906, she volunteered to join a group of doctors and nurses who provided emergency care to victims of the San Francisco Earthquake and Fire. The California Governor, San Francisco Mayor and U.S. Army authorities praised her efforts.

During this stage of her life and medical practice, she publicly avowed two unpopular and illegal social positions: contraception and abortion. Unlikely many practitioners, she evaded serious consequences for her actions. Most observers have suggested that because hers was a general practice and not focused solely on performing abortions, authorities overlooked her activities.

Equi initiated one of her longest-term romantic relationships with the younger Harriet Speckart, the niece of Olympic Brewing Company founder Leopold Schmidt. Speckart's family disapproved of their union obliging her to wrestle in court for years with her mother and brother over her rightful inheritance upon her father's death. Equi and Speckart adopted and raised an infant girl, making their partnership distinctive for the era.

In 1912, Equi's character was first called into question regarding a dispute at her medical office. She was involved in a physical altercation with the building's superintendent. Her medical practice was being evicted for an unspecified reason and she was allegedly caught rifling through files in another doctor's office. She engaged in a fight with the building's superintendent prompting a police visit. The superintendent was arrested but later acquitted at his trial. Unconfirmed reports surfaced that Equi was a known blackmailer. A presumption circulated that she was seeking potential blackmail documents from other doctor's files. This accusation would be repeated publicly six years later during her own arrest and public trial. Was this reputation accurate?

One could easily conclude that in an antagonistic society hostile to your lifestyle, politics and medical agenda, aggressive tactics were necessary. If she was obliged to fight enemy fire with equal ferocity, then blackmailing local officials were an incidental price. Much of her ammunition came from abortions that she had performed on behalf of police officials.

Marie Equi's social concerns became more radicalized when she visited a cannery worker strike at the Oregon Packing Company. The protesting workers, predominately women, rallied against the poor working conditions, wages and erratic work shifts. She joined the protest and became one of its leaders based on the respect given to her professional stature. Following days of tireless picketing, police finally charged the strikers. Police dragged a 30-year-old pregnant woman away from the procession. Equi became enraged and was clubbed by an officer. This intimate experience with police brutality altered her former progressive politics into more extreme political views.

The strike ended unsuccessfully for the workers, but Marie Equi aligned her politics with the Radical Socialist and Anarchist movements. A wave of nationalism had swept America prior to entering World War I. She considered American involvement *a grab for profits by capitalists and an imperialistic adventure for the government.*

Equi's aggressive pacifism and extreme distrust towards Capitalist motives isolated her. These solitary protests against the current of mainstream popular sentiment made her vulnerable to physical violence and arrest. In 1918, she was charged with sedition under a newly modified Espionage Act forbidding criticism of the U.S. Government, Constitution, military, flag, navy and/or uniforms. Ironically she often recruited ex-soldiers to distribute her pamphlets and literature because they were unafraid of being confronted by the Portland police.

At her trial, Equi's lawyers produced an impressive roster of prominent citizens including Governor Oswald West to speak on her behalf. Their surprise participation fueled the suspicion and rumors that she had damaging blackmail material against each advocate for her cause.

The prosecution spared no delicacies and savagely smeared her reputation and sexuality. An obliging jury convicted her on December 31, 1918 and sentenced her to three-years imprisonment. The war had already concluded the previous month on November 11th. President Woodrow Wilson would commute her sentence to one year and a day shortly before his death.

She appealed the decision but lost the following year. In 1920, she served ten months at San Quentin as the sole political prisoner. She was incarcerated with thirty-eight other women interned for murder, theft and performing abortions.

She left prison suffering from a return flare-up of tuberculosis that she had contracted in childhood. Radical political movements were effective shattered by the conclusion of the war. Many of her comrades remained imprisoned or restricted against protest activity due to a sweeping fear of post-war communist infiltration.

Equi continued her medical practice, but led a more serene existence. She separated from Speckart. Her daughter Mary eloped and later became the first female pilot in Oregon. She hosted Elizabeth Gurley Flynn, leader of the Industrial Workers of the World (IWW) during her recovery from am intense bout depression and exhaustion.

In 1950, she fractured her hip in a fall and was hospitalized for an entire year recuperating. She then relocated to a nursing home in nearby Gresham where she died at Fairlawn Hospital on July 13, 1952 at the age of 80.

There are numerous contributing factors that prevented Marie Equi from achieving national icon status. Her anti-war imprisonment, sexual preference and real or imagined status as a blackmailer were perhaps too extreme to qualify for societal sainthood.

One may disagree with her political conclusions, but one should never dismiss or disregard the courage and compassion that she steadfastly exhibited during an era when she refused to accept second-class citizenry status or simply remain complacently silent.

Dr. Marie Equi's Residences:
Nortonia Hotel (currently Mark Spencer Hotel), 409
SW 11th Avenue, Portland
Hotel Oregon, Formerly Corner of SW Broadway and
SW Harvey Milk Street, Portland (Demolished)

**Dr. Marie Equi's Medical Practice:
Lafayette Building, Corner of Sixth and Washington,
Portland (Demolished)
The Medical Building, 729 SW Alder Street, Portland**

Richards Restaurant and Clandestine Booth Service(s)

The same Richards Hotel and Restaurant, Alder Park Shoppes and currently named Galt Building were constructed in 1904. Lauritz Therkelsen, a Danish immigrant who arrived in Portland in 1871 after ten years residence in San Francisco, originally owned the structure. As a carpenter and contractor, Therkelsen built numerous residential and commercial structures making his firm the city's largest. He was a successful entrepreneur owning the North Pacific Lumber Company and a shrewd local real estate investor.

Designed in the Twentieth Century Classical style, the edifice features a metal tile roof and modillions at the roof cornice. Blind arches of cement plaster on the walls are featured with a panel effect under the windows and a belt course above the ground floor.

Originally operating as the Richards Hotel, the property featured telephones, baths and luxurious hot and cold water in every room. Thomas Richards operated the hotel and adjoining restaurant reputed to be a front for prostitution.

The restaurant featured side entrances where fine cuisine, wines and choice liquors were served. Clandestine booths and intimate dining rooms leading off from the narrow corridors accommodated higher priced illicit commerce. Two-term mayor Harry Lane launched a crusade to close the restaurant and others similarly designed. Thomas Richards evaded legal prosecution, but not scandal. Debt forced him to lose his liquor license and the establishment in 1914.

The three-story building was enlarged and remodeled in 1922 with an additional construction directly behind the original edifice. The building was renamed the Alder Park Shoppes in 1926 to accommodate commercial establishments on the upper floors. The complex has historically featured hospitality, retail and financial industry tenants.

The current Galt Building's moniker is derived from *John Galt*, the lead character in Ayn Rand's best-known novel *Atlas Shrugged*. Its distinctive cobalt blue exterior distinguishes it boldly within a neighborhood of architectural conformity.

Galt Building
800-808 SW Alder Street, Portland

Washington Hotel's Lavender Heritage

Architect Lionel Deane designed the original five-story Washington Hotel in 1911 in the Renaissance Revival style. Detailed brickwork and a heavy cornice band highlight the upper four residential floors while the ground level is a mix of materials that has been altered following over a century of use and design modifications. From the outset, the bottom floor featured a tavern with Deane listed as the original saloonkeeper in the 1912 Portland City Directory.

Deane was born in 1861 in Canada and began studying architecture at the age of sixteen. He arrived in Portland in 1889 and worked for the firm of Justus Krumbein. In 1899, he moved to San Francisco and professionally partnered for four years with James Kollofrath. Following the devastating 1906 Earthquake and Fire, he became active in reconstruction projects.

He returned to Portland in 1911 to work on the Washington Hotel project. Deane was outed and arrested as one of the more prominent homosexuals during the 1912 Vice Clique Scandal. He resigned from his California affiliation and moved to New York City. By 1920, he was licensed to practice in New York State where he remained until his death in 1938.

The lower level tavern became a prominent gay bar called the *Timber Topper* between 1970-1974, the *Axe Handle* (1974) and finally *The Alley*. The entrance remained situated on 428 SW Twelfth Avenue and currently hosts the Ruby Jewel Ice Cream parlor. Today the hotel has been modified to the Washington Apartments offering both temporary and permanent accommodations.

Washington Hotel (renamed Washington Apartments)
1129 SW Washington Street, Portland

Portland's Vice Clique Gay Subculture Scandal of 1912

The arrest of nineteen-year old male prostitute Benjamin Trout on November 12, 1912 initiated the *Vice Clique Scandal* alerting Portland law enforcement authorities and the general public that an illegal gay male subculture existed within the city.

Trout was arrested for shoplifting but parlayed his interrogation into a pronouncement that *he had been corrupted by a number of men in town*. How his interpretation applied towards his shoplifting arrest evaded explanation.

His revelations provided police with an unregulated license to conduct a *sodomy* roundup that penetrated into several notable public officials, medical officials and legal professionals. Constitutional, consensual and privacy rights were ignored and violated stimulated by a mania to cleanse the community of *indecent acts*. Sixty-eight men were identified as being involved in the sex scandal.

The purge was wholeheartedly supported by *The Portland News* and its editor Dana Sleeth and Congressman Walter Lafferty who vowed to expand the scandal's momentum into Washington DC. The Oregon state legislature responded to the hysteria by clarifying and strengthening the state's anti-sodomy laws and making the act punishable by sterilization. A measure of sanity ultimately prevailed as Oregon voters approved a referendum that repealed the sterilization measure by a majority of 56% percent.

The most visible member of the Vice Clique was attorney Edward McAllister who was charged with committing an *immoral act* with Roy Kadel in his law office. McAllister had met Kadel and a companion on a busy Portland thoroughfare and invited them into his reception room. He ushered Kadel into his private office for an extended period. Kadel's impatient companion, who claimed he had unwittingly accompanied his friend, interrupted the conclusion of Kadel's sexual ejaculation upon storming into the room.

A month later, an arrest warrant was issued for McAllister who was in Coos Bay that day taking depositions for a legal case. He vowed to return to Portland to face charges, but was arrested on a southbound train heading towards California two days later.

His subsequent trial became a public crusade and condemnation against homosexuality. The district attorney condemned *those addicted to the practice of sodomy or the crime against nature and other gross, bestial and perverted sexual habits and practices prohibited by statute.*

McAllister's background was intriguing beginning with his middle name, which was *Stonewall Jackson* even though he'd been born in Maryland in 1867. He was a Methodist and Congregational clergyman between 1894-1904 before becoming a lawyer in Portland in 1904. He became an assistant to Judge W. D. Fenton, a former Southern Pacific Railroad attorney and the namesake of his law building. He married Margaret Wiley from Bainbridge, Pennsylvania in 1898, but divorced before his arrival to Portland. He was casually nicknamed *Mother McAllister* due to his reputation of overtly soliciting men for sex on the street and his popular hunting grounds, Lownsdale Square.

At trial, a string of sexual partners testified against him (presumably in return for immunity). He was found guilty and sentenced between one to five years in the state penitentiary. This judgment was considered *lenient* considering the standard sentence was five years, later tripled to fifteen by the state legislature. Physician Harry Start and bookkeeper Edward Wedemeyer were also handed prison sentences during their publicly followed trials. All three appealed their convictions.

The Oregon Supreme Court reversed all three convictions based on legal technicalities and prejudicial practices imposed by Judge John Kavanaugh on the jury.

McAllister, who'd considered running for a judgeship just before the scandal broke, never recovered his previous professional esteem or former political clout. He attempted to re-establish his law practice afterwards despite his partner's dissolution of the firm and supported himself as a legal clerk. His reputation beyond repair, he left Portland in 1915 and settled in the town of Myrtle Creek in Douglas County as a farmer. He successfully petitioned the Oregon Supreme Court in 1921 to direct the state to reimburse him for the costs of his trial defense. He died five years later of a stroke at the age of 58. In 2000, the Multnomah Bar Association posthumously reinstated McAllister citing the sole reason for his earlier expulsion was having been gay.

One of the more ironic victims emerging from the scandal was Portland's YMCA where some of the accused males resided. Portland's organization was the ninth largest in North America, and the largest membership in the United States, strongly supported financially by the city's elite. The organization and its sponsors were viciously attacked by some of the local news media, motivated perhaps by a suspicion they had done nothing to squelch and monitor the *immorally* perceived practice. At the conclusion of the frenzy, it was determined that only four men in the scandal actually lived in the building with two others previously residing there.

In the midst of disclosure, several local businesses were exposed as homosexual nesting locations including:

The ABC restaurant located within the downtown Palace Hotel (since demolished)

Hotel San Marco where Harry Work, a desk clerk was arrested. He would provide damaging evidence against McAllister during his trial (demolished in 1999)

Imperial Hotel (currently the Hotel Lucia) where the first floor lobby restroom was a popular male companionship meeting location. After the Vice Clique Scandal, the newly formed Portland Social Hygiene Society mandated elevator operators and bellhops to receive sexual hygiene training

The Louvre Café located within the downtown Belvedere Hotel featuring a grill segregated exclusively for men (demolished in the late 1940s)

Lownsdale Square, originally segregated by city ordinance for males only. The brick rest room had a particularly poor reputation.

YMCA Building featuring individual rooms with telephone connections to the building switchboard, but no private bathrooms. The YMCA created a *Strangers' Club* and weekly socials to enable new men in town to make friends and establish a social contact base (demolished in 1978)

Moffitt Photographic Studio where proprietor John Moffitt was arrested during the scandal. He promoted his notoriety advertising his services as a *Photographer of Men,* ideal for discreet same-sex couples (building demolished in 1977)

Orpheum Theatre, the balcony was renowned as a gathering place for a *certain class of patron* (demolished in 1977)

Whitney-Gray Apartments, residence of Earle Van Hulen whose sexual encounter with Edward Wedemeyer led to the latter's indictment and trial

Fenton Building, law offices of McAllister and Upton in suites 409-412. Edward McAllister's private office was the site of his notorious sexual tryst with Roy Kadel (demolished and replaced in 1948 by the Commonwealth Building)

One of the most tragic casualties from the Vice Clique Scandal was the fate of Edwin *Sid* Ghirardelli, from the famed San Francisco chocolate and mustard family. Ghirardelli was gay and had been banished to Portland by his parents to avoid family embarrassment from his San Francisco based lovers. He was the sole family member to have never worked for the company.

A position had been arranged for him in Portland with a merchandise broker firm. His boss was aware of the cause for his banishment, but fired him anyway for *lapsed behavior* in December 1912 as the Vice Clique trials began. Simultaneous letters sent by Ghirardelli and his former boss to his family met collective hostile reaction from his father, mother and brother. Each expressed shame and a stern rebuke against him ever returning home.

He became despondent over their reaction and limped through his December 27th birthday in utter despair. During the final week of 1912, he squandered his remaining money with other men in a Turkish bathhouse. He took a cab back to his room #412 in the Byron Hotel and swallowed lethal poison that he had purchased earlier. His body was discovered on New Years Day, 1913 by concerned hotel employees who had not seen him and were aware of his mental state. The Byron Hotel, once located on the SE corner of Broadway and Salmon Streets was demolished in December 1959. Edwin *Sid* Ghirardelli's unpleasant fate and circumstances remain in obscurity.

Imperial Hotel (currently the Hotel Lucia)
400 SW Broadway, Portland

**Whitney-Gray Apartments
409 SW Twelfth Avenue, Portland**

Crystal Ballroom: Dancing On Clouds For Over A Century

Portland's Crystal Ballroom was constructed in 1914 and has weathered two crises of local controversy beginning from its outset. Operating as the Cotillion Hall, original owner Montrose Ringler promoted jazz acts and dancing until the early 1920s when local authorities intervened and shut down the venue. Their principle fury was directed towards the publicly perceived lewd dances and moves the music provoked.

Part of their complaint may have stemmed from a unique flooring system patented in 1905 stimulating the sensation of floating or dancing on a cloud. Around the perimeter of the floor are ratchet holes where the tension of the floor can be altered, depending on the intended dance. The unusual rocker-and-ball design was originally intended for ballroom dancing, but has accommodated decades of evolving dance styles.

Ringler lost ownership of the ballroom during the early 1920s and it was purchased shortly afterwards by Dad Watson who limited events to square dances. Upon his death in the 1930s, Ralph Farrier purchased the hall and renamed it the Crystal Ballroom. He continued the square dances until the late 1950s. Farrier died days after presiding over a final New Year's dance. The direction of bookings changed radically with fresh ownership.

During the early 1960s, R & B and soul music performing acts headlined. They included James Brown, Marvin Gaye, Ike and Tina Turner, Wilson Pickett and Etta James. A fanciful story circulated that during an April 1965 show, singer Little Richard fired Jimi Hendrix on stage during a performance. Although Hendrix was part of his touring band that year, the story has never been substantiated by any other source than rumor and the current owner's marketing literature.

The psychedelic rock era in the late 1960s appeared at the Crystal Ballroom for a brief eighteen months before stimulating enough local hysteria to shut it down once again. City building inspectors flunked the ballroom for numerous code violations. The greatest local fear then was Portland becoming a major *hippie satellite* of San Francisco. Among the more renowned acts performing included the Grateful Dead, Jefferson Airplane and Buffalo Springfield.

During the 1970s through mid-1990s, the ballroom remained dark for pubic events and became a squatter's residence and artist studio space. A fire on June 24, 1988 caused extensive damage to the building and interior contents.

In 1997, the McMenamins ownership group re-opened the venue featuring a ground floor restaurant and bar, second level dance floor and third level main ballroom. The flooring remains the same.

TWISTED TOUR GUIDES.com

Crystal Ballroom
1332 W Burnside Street, Portland

Emma Goldman: The Validity of a Lecture Series Over A Century Later

Portland's Turn Verein Hall became the site of political activist Emma Goldman's famed August 1915 lecture series. Goldman toured the United States speaking on controversial subjects including birth control, socialism, Russian drama, Frederick Nietzsche and *The Intermediate Sex* (homosexuality).

Turnverein is German for *Gymnastics Club*. The facility was informally known locally as the *Scandinavian Socialists Hall*.

Goldman's lectures were advertised and scrupulously covered by The *Oregonian* newspaper. Controversy surrounded her local arrest on charges of distributing *obscene* birth control literature.

Her presentations stirred up local reaction as probably no speaker before or since. Critics cited her propaganda of atheism, anarchy and free love as a defiant challenge to the fundamentals of American society. Censorship made Goldman bolder. Her defense of lifestyle choices without society's stigmatization made her message as sensible and pertinent then as over a century later.

Throughout her life, Goldman stimulated debate. In 1917, she was sentenced to two years in jail for inducing American males not to register for the draft. After her release, she was deported to Russia where she initially became a vocal supporter of the Bolshevik revolution. She left the Soviet Union in 1923 disillusioned with their government for its violent repression of independent voices. She died in 1940 at the age of 70 in Toronto, Canada both admired and detested; yet never silenced.

The Turn Verein Hall was ultimately demolished and present day site is the downtown Pioneer Place Building.

Former Turn Verein Hall Site
Pioneer Place Building, 700 SW Fifth Avenue, Portland

Hatred and Portland's 1920s Ku Klux Klan Infatuation

Beatrice Morrow Cannady became Portland's most visible civil rights advocate during the early twentieth century. She was editor of the *Advocate,* the state's largest African-American newspaper and co-founder and Vice President of Portland's chapter of the NAACP.

During August 1915, promoters of the film *The Birth of a Nation* petitioned the Portland city council for the right to show the film in the city. Cannady became the loudest voice of reason against the petition with her famous words *As Citizens of Portland We Must Protest.* Her declaration was based on the certainty that the film was *not only historically untrue, but that it incited hatred between the races.* Her futile plea was timely, but ignored in every American city where the film was shown.

The Birth of a Nation was a silent movie about the Civil War, Reconstruction, and the rise of the Ku Klux Klan. The controversial film required eight months to shoot, featured a cast of eighteen thousand and cost a staggering half a million dollars, ten times its initial budget.

The screenplay was adapted from the novel and play *The Clansman* and the film directed by D. W. Griffith. The movie stereotyped freed slaves as a menace to the *New South* portraying hooded members of the Klan as the *saviors* of American civilization. It required three hours to view and twelve reels to contain. Admission was set at an unprecedented price with reserved seating mandated for twice daily showings at the Heilig Theatre on SW Broadway Street.

Portlanders displayed their moral indifference by packing the theatre throughout its initial run. A later 1922 showing achieved similar popularity. Griffith chafed under the criticism from the NAACP requested boycott of the film. He defiantly maintained that he had *nothing* to apologize for. His clueless response was the film *Intolerance* that he produced the following year. The movie received lavish praise for its elaborate costuming, sets and technical innovations. The laborious three and a half hours required to sit through it did not register nearly the commercial and financial acclaim as *The Birth of a Nation*.

Hatred and overt racism continued to make front-page headlines locally.

On August 1, 1921, two members of the local Ku Klux Klan in full regalia staged a surprise photo bomb with some of Portland's most recognized civic and law enforcement leaders at the Multnomah Hotel. A posed group shot of the local leaders was reputedly set up absent of the clansman. Both appeared from behind a background curtain seconds before the photographer snapped the shot. One aligned himself in the center of the group and the other at the eastern extremity.

The photo appeared in the *Portland Telegram* the following day with the headline: *Chief Kluxers Tell Law Enforcement Officers Just What Mystic Organization Proposes To Do In City of Portland*. The prominent inclusions in the infamous photo included police chief Leon Jenkins, Sheriff Thomas Hurlburt, District Attorney Lester Humphries and Mayor George Baker.

The KKK used the publicity stunt as a recruiting tool to insinuate their alleged influence with civic leaders. Klan membership was reputed to be popular amongst members of the police bureau. Given the organization's paranoia towards secrecy and membership ranks, the claim was difficult to substantiate. Their publicly avowed agenda of *100% American* strikes a chilling comparison with contemporary political movements and rhetoric.

During the early 1920s, candidates with Klan endorsements began winning key local elected positions. Their platform of reforming an existing corrupt system proved ironic. Candidates Dow Walker and John Rankin won positions in 1924 on the Multnomah County Planning Commission joining existing Chairman Charles Rudeen. Both candidates vowed to reform the county's operations involving public construction projects.

Their initial test came with the 1924 voter's approval of a $5 million bond issue to replace the Burnside Bridge and construct two additional bridges designed to relieve growing traffic congestion.

The resulting bridge scandal verified the hypocrisy behind their platforms. Bidding for the three bridge projects was restricted to a single day, but still generated two bids. Walker, Rankin and Rudeen voted unanimously to accept a three-bridge construction package bid even though it was substantially higher. The losing bidder sued the county and a state initiated audit uncovered that the three commissioners had split a significant cash payoff from the winning bidder. One commissioner had profited handsomely from purchasing strategic lots on the east side of the bridge location at an undervalued price.

When news of the bridge scandal became public, each of the three commissioners was disgraced and recalled. The reputation of the Klan also suffered due to their complicity with electing the members.

The actual influence of the organization proved debatable.

The Klan publicized grand ambitions to expand their Portland base initially establishing an office in the Pittock Building. Leaders announced plans to construct a ten-story building downtown. Construction never materialized due to the Depression and the bridge scandal slowed their political agenda significantly. At the conclusion of World War II, the organization enjoyed a brief upswing in popularity statewide. Their perceived level of influence within Portland circles would never be duplicated.

Infamous *Portland Telegram* KKK Photo With City Officials

**Former Heilig Theatre Site
(currently) Fox Tower, 805 SW Broadway Street,
Portland**

1924 Burnside Bridge Construction Scandal

**Former Offices of Portland's Ku Klux Klan Chapter
Pittock Block, 921 SW Washington Street**

Golden West Hotel: A Lingering Landmark From The Failed Prohibition Era

During the first half of the twentieth century, a Pullman Railroad porter was one of the most prestigious jobs for an African American male. With Oregon's implementation of Prohibition on January 1, 1916 (four years before the 18th Amendment), the liquor distribution network went underground. Railroad porters evolved into some of the most efficient and prolific bootleggers.

A secret society called the *Brotherhood of Sleeping Car Porters* coordinated local operations that became adept with their smuggling techniques and inventive bribing of police officers. Their headquarters operated out of the Golden West Hotel conveniently located nearby Union Station.

The Golden West was constructed in 1890 and was originally known as the Tremont House. William D. Allen and his silent partner Al Wohlers purchased the Tremont in 1906 and renamed it the *Golden West* the following year. It became known for inexpensive lodgings catering to railroad workers and was the first integrated hotel locally.

In 1912, a fifth floor penthouse level was added providing contemporary and luxurious suites. Chauffeurs and particularly porters, many of whom were also known bootleggers, occupied the suites. Their significant cash earnings enabled a flashy lifestyle.

Silent partner Wohlers was an ex-policeman, saloonkeeper, pimp and reputed conduit between the Northern Portland vice businesses and law enforcement agencies. Following a series of prostitution raids at the Golden West in 1907,

Wohlers negotiated a financial agreement with law enforcement and the property evaded police harassment for the next decade.

Prohibition and the emerging expansion of the porter-bootlegging ring brought fresh surveillance and scrutiny to the property. A highly publicized 1917 IRS raid netted a significant cache of whiskey from the penthouse occupants. One of the residents, Dave Thornton was rumored to be running a speakeasy from his suite. Thornton would die mysteriously two years later from a self-inflicted gun wound. The largest haul would originate from leader John Lowe's room resulting in his immediate arrest. Lowe would later be implicated in various criminal enterprises and be sentenced to life in prison.

The Southern Pacific Railroad network, originating from the Canadian border where the illegal spirits were produced until San Diego proved ideal. The porter's stiffest competition came from local law enforcement that protected their own chosen distributors.

Inventory arriving at Union Station would be collected in trunks from the baggage department. A porter would load the cargo into his cart and wheel it across the waiting room to the front door. If an officer was suspicious of the baggage, they would employ a *shake and sniff test*, absent of a search warrant. After seizing and dropping the containers, officers would then listen for telltale gurgling or sniffed whiskey fumes from broken bottles.

Police seized significant quantities of illegal booze, but many of the subsequent legal cases were later tossed out of court based on violations of search and seizure laws. When the Union Station depot began to accumulate too many seizures, porters began unloading cargo at rural train stations. The contraband would then be driven into Portland by car.

Throughout the entire evasion dance and charade, the Southern Pacific and baggage officials refused to cooperate fully with law enforcement organizations.

During this era, the police department's vice squad charge was enforcing local alcohol, prostitution and gambling laws selectively. The squad targeted *unauthorized* vice operators; those who didn't pay for police protection. Successive police chiefs made overtures towards cleaning up the entrenched network, but the corruption ran deep. Mayor George Baker used confiscated liquor intended for trial evidence as his own personal inventory. Throughout his multiple terms, Prohibition was in full effect. The majority of publicized raids and arrests targeted the lower end of the distribution chain.

Within its first year of enforcement, it became clear Prohibition was a total failure. Consumption had not decreased significantly, cities were losing considerable revenue from liquor licensing and taxation and a fresh criminal element was emerging. Law enforcement became compromised and corrupt by protection payments.

The quest for leadership of the porter's ring was violent and bloodied by a major challenge to the throne. The first acknowledged leader was *Yam* Wallace. An intervention and embarrassing assault by a competing Kansas City faction left Wallace vulnerable. One of his working distributors, Tom Johnson exploited the opportunity.

The two had a falling out in 1921 and during an altercation, Johnson, a World War I veteran, drew a knife and cut Wallace severely requiring his hospitalization. Soon afterwards, Wallace was arrested with nearly $10,000 worth of cocaine in his possession. He was given a sentence of life imprisonment that cleared the way for Johnson's leadership.

Under Johnson's reign, the bootlegging ring continued to thrive for the next twenty years. He was savvy enough to diversify his own investments into real estate holdings and nightclubs. His clubs were noteworthy for incomparable after-hours jam sessions featuring headliners such as Louis Armstrong, Duke Ellington and Billie Holiday.

Johnson prudently negotiated truces with law enforcement, city officials and competitors. He expanded his political base and wealth being one of the few facilitators for African-American housing. Over the decades, he minimized his formative criminal past and was lionized as a distinguished community leader absent of notoriety upon his death.

The Golden West continued hotel operations until 1931 when the Great Depression cut into railroad employment and forced the property's closure. The building was sold in 1933 and briefly reopened as the *New Golden West Hotel* for two years. More ownership changes followed until 1943 when the building became the Broadmoor Hotel, a low-cost housing development that continued until 1984. At the beginning of the Millennium, the property was renamed back to the more celebrated Golden West Hotel. It continues to function as low-end housing offering 68 units for mentally ill residents and single-room occupancy.

Union Station
800 NW Sixth Avenue, Portland

Golden West Hotel, 707 NW Everett Street, Portland

The 1917 Mayor's Election That Tilted Portland to the Right

The 1917 Portland mayoral election was shaping up to be a pivotal vote that ultimately would determine the course of the city political scene for the next two decades. City councilman George Baker was a former theatre owner with the full support of local business interests and the then dominant Republican Party. His strongest opponent and the election favorite was Will H. Daly, also a registered Republican, but whose base included strong support from a coalition of Democratic and Progressive Party activists. Daly had served as the head of the Oregon Labor Federation, a member of the Portland Central Labor Council and as an official of the Typographical Union.

The wildcard in this election was Henry Lewis Pittock, Oregon's equivalent of William Randolph Hearst who was influential politically and the founder and publisher of *The Oregonian*, the state's preeminent daily newspaper.

Daly and Pittock were well acquainted. Daly had been a linotype operator at *The Oregonian* until 1911. His union activities became a nuisance to Pittock, but their relationship evolved into personal animosity when Daly was appointed as Portland's Utility Commissioner. Daly had forced the installation of water meters for all local customers and exposed a corrupt deal between Pittock and the city to provide a pipeline of water at city expense to Pittock's hilltop mansion. His property was located in excess of a mile outside of the city limits.

Pittock feared that a Daly election would prove adverse to his interests and actively campaigned against him via his newspaper with smear tactics that arguably swayed the election. Among the paper's most inflammatory claims was that Daly was a labor agitator, threat to the war effort and the local shipbuilding industry and the most damning, a Socialist Party member.

On June 2, 1917, three days before the election, Daly's home was burglarized. Valuables were ignored but Daly's personal papers were scanned thoroughly. Missing was an uncompleted application for Socialist Party membership dated 1910.

The following day a photo of the stolen application mysteriously appeared in *The Oregonian* under a headline *Daly Socialist Since 1910*. The same issue featured a front-page editorial by Pittock portrayed as news, stressing that Daly was a security threat to Portland due to his political views.

Pittock's questionable ethical tactics prevailed. His media propaganda barrage shifted a once certain Daly victory into a slim George Baker election. Portland's existing commercial and political interests remained status quo. Baker would serve as mayor from 1917 to 1933 and oversee a period of rampant corruption, growth of organized crime and unparalleled antagonism against union activities. He is considered one of Portland's worst and most compromised mayors and became largely forgotten upon his death in May 1941.

Pittock's Machiavellian maneuverings during the 1917 election became one of his final successful schemes. Two years later, he would become stricken by influenza and die on January 28, 1919. He managed the newspaper and his personal financial affairs until days before his death. On the night before he died, he was carried to an east bay window of his mansion to gaze upon the city where he had amassed a fortune and elevated and squashed careers. His estate was the largest ever probated in Oregon at that time.

His French Renaissance-style chateau was designed by San Francisco architect Edward Foulkes on 46 acres in 1909. The family remained on the property after his death. Damage during the severe 1962 Columbus Day storm nearly prompted the buildings demolition. The property was purchased by the City of Portland in 1964 and is currently operated by the Bureau of Parks and Recreation.

The since popular tourist attraction offers a stunning panoramic view of downtown and is terraced with gorgeous landscaped gardens. Accompanying the beauty, visitors have reported viewing disembodied voices, phantom footsteps, apparitions and window latches that have mysteriously come undone. The active spirits and paranormal activity have been attributed to members of the departed Pittock Family.

Henry Pittock's alleged improprieties, abuse of power and scandals have been largely sanitized over time. The age of singular wealthy local power brokers has diminished. Newspapers wield significantly less influence than in 1917. It is certain that contemporary Portland politics would be odious to Henry Pittock and his political perspectives.

TWISTED TOUR GUIDES.com

Will H. Daly Residence, 3605 North Missouri Avenue

Pittock Mansion, 3229 NW Pittock Drive, Portland

Crime Hotel Incorporated and The Vortex of Vice

The Read Hotel was located across the street from Lownsdale Square between 1909 and 1967. The building was a non-descript residential hotel with distinctive secrets. During the 1930s, the Read was reputed to be a gathering point and haven for burglars, armed robbers, kidnappers and ex-convicts. In such an environment, fugitives from justice habitually sought refuge. The script and casting oozing from the property resembled a Film Noir movie.

During prohibition, resident bootleggers purchased protection from potentially prying law enforcement agencies, eager for their percentage of the illicit enterprise. Jean Miller, a heroin addict and member of a prominent local family, operated the Read. Rumors circulated that Miller through her attorney had insulated the hotel from police interference since 1918.

Even with the payoffs, periodic arrests for bootlegging, beatings and prostitution were not uncommon at the property.

One of the more storied local robberies was the popular Birdlegs Roadhouse owned by *Birdlegs* Reed, a blind African American gambler and club owner. *Birdlegs* had formerly operated the Union Club (since demolished) before establishing his suburban roadhouse away from prying local surveillance. On December 20, 1926, two armed men robbed the facility, gagging and tying up the customers before stealing their cash and jewelry. One of those customers was John Lowe, a rival of *Birdlegs* coincidentally patronizing his establishment that evening.

A few days following the robbery, Fay B. Wise (no kidding) and Neil Anderson were apprehended. Both had long criminal records for burglary. Both were coincidentally residents of the Read Hotel. Wise's protestation that he was *going straight* following his arrest fooled no one within the law enforcement fraternity. What came as a minor surprise was that both men implicated John Lowe as the orchestrator of the heist. Lowe had a long history with legal entanglements and formerly headed one of the largest bootlegging operations on the West Coast. He'd evaded numerous attempts on his own life. He was eventually sentenced to twenty years in the Oregon State Penitentiary ending his career of local mayhem. Wise and Anderson returned to their too familiar prison accommodations.

Fay B. Wise had profited little from his continued illegal activities. Follow his subsequent release from prison four years later, he returned to his Read Hotel residence and once again was arrested for burglary piling on an additional four years of incarceration.

Upon this release in 1935, Wise upped the ante of criminal suspicion by becoming a prime suspect in the murder of destitute Ada Haskins, a co-resident at the Read. On July 25, 1936, Haskins was found strangled to death with a piece of baling wire. Astute Portland investigators initially suspected that her death might be *suicide*. Rationality briefly prevailed and the nearby luckless Wise seemed a more probable suspect.

Haskins had recently gone through a divorce apparently over a sexually transmitted disease. Her ex-husband had committed suicide. She had lent Wise and another ex-convict $100 each with the IOU's due on the date of her death. Haskins reportedly had dressed to impress that evening for a date with two men. Her expectations proved fruitless upon her strangulation in her room. The police, lacking conclusive evidence, irrationally concluded that she had killed herself. Local reaction was indifferent and only her distant family vainly protested the verdict,

A continuing litany of crime and suspected lawlessness emanated from Read Hotel residents over the subsequent decades. Two well-known incidents involved the July 1938 kidnapping and ransom of a visiting Idaho farmer and September 1947 fatal beating of Ethel Jane Rice by Rutherford Beer. In 1938, proprietress Jean Miller was convicted of harboring fugitives. Her infamous attorney I.G. Ankles would be disbarred in 1934 following charges of forgery. He was reinstated in 1938 and permanently disbarred the same year for operating an extortion ring from the hotel.

The neighborhood worsened during the 1950s and the Read Hotel personified the decline. Operations continued until 1967 when it was shuttered permanently and later demolished. Yesterday's *vortex of vice* became yet another downtown parking facility and ground level store outlet. The criminal class simply found it necessary to spread their ranks to other sectors of town.

Former Location of Reading Hotel
(currently City Center Parking)
920 SW Fourth Avenue, Portland

From The Great Depression Until Today: Where Do All The Homeless Go?

Portland, like every other American urban center is struggling with the issue of unwelcome and unpermitted homeless habitats. The latest twist has been a policy of encouraging camping pup tents that proliferate the downtown, North End, waterfront and public parks. By nightfall, Portland becomes a veritable tent city seemingly at odds with the current period of economic prosperity.

The roots of the issue go back decades to the Great Depression and shantytowns that sprung up in the Sullivan's Gulch district and under the west end of the Ross Island Bridge. The *Hoovervilles* were named after the very unpopular Republican President Herbert Hoover. At present, the tent encampments have evaded *Trumpesque* monikers.

The shantytowns were generally neighborhoods of shacks made from scrap wood, car parts, corrugated tin and cardboard boxes. The villages had its own elected mayor, commissary and post office. Residents paid taxes by serving on garbage collection patrols. The Ross Island Bridge settlement had a community Finnish steam bath and a flushing toilet that drained into the Willamette River. The Sullivan's Gulch shantytown had a telephone much to the envy of other local settlements.

The Dairy Cooperative Association provided fresh milk deliveries and the settlement mayor made the rounds of nearby bakeries, grocery and clothing stores to collect donations.

The primary objective for the residents from the outset of the *Hoovervilles* was to find employment. As the

Depression began to end and war related employment rose, the shantytown populations began to diminish. By 1941, the settlements became deserted and fires burned what remained into ashes.

The occupied land in Sullivan's Gulch had been the object of a feasibility study for an auto expressway as early as 1926. In 1947, the state highway commission approved plans for a freeway that ultimately upon construction became Interstate 84.

Sullivan's Gulch Hoovervilles
Interstate 84, Portland

A Singular Voice of Pacifist Dissent Crushed

Assistant Portland City Librarian Louise Hunt became an incidental casualty in the patriotic mania following America's entry into World War I. Hunt was born in Portland, Maine and arrived locally via Philadelphia's Drexel Institute and the Lansing, Michigan public library. In 1917, the Portland Central Library was considered one of the finest on the West Coast.

Before America's entry into the war, Hunt made a trip to Washington D.C. to lobby Oregon's congressional delegation into maintaining American soldiers stateside. Her position had formerly been consistent with President Woodrow Wilson's who was re-elected in 1916 based on his resolve to keep American troops out of the conflict.

By 1917, Wilson's perspective had altered, but Hunt's had not. Her visit to Washington was received with hostility. Once America entered the war, she kept her unpopular opinions to herself and focused on her job. A pacifist amidst the national war clamor was an endangered and targeted species.

Public libraries committed their operations towards the war efforts, providing current information and war news, civilian training in conjunction with the Red Cross and reading materials for army bases and hospitals. They removed books that were considered pro-German or promoted pacifism. They sold War Savings Stamps and Liberty Bonds. Hunt was assigned to staff a War Stamp kiosk in the Central Library's lobby. She fulfilled her obligation to sell stamps, but refused to purchase any herself.

In April 1917, the library board of directors received an anonymous letter accusing Hunt of disloyalty based on her personal lack of purchased stamps and bonds. The board investigated the charges and after Head Librarian Mary Isom testified to her loyalty and employee diligence, they cleared her of wrongdoing.

One Board member was unsatisfied by the verdict and leaked the anonymous letter and board's decision to the press. A media firestorm followed creating a public scandal and pointed denouncement from Mayor George Baker.

The solitary right of Louise Hunt's silent dissent was crushed. She resigned her position and returned back to her family home in Maine.

Portland Central Public Library
801 SW Tenth Avenue, Portland

Henry Albers: Poorly Timed Overindulgence and Serenading

Bernard Albers arrived into Portland in 1889 after emigrating from Lingen, Germany. He began employment as a driver for a feed merchant company, an industry his father had trained him in. Wheat and flour were two of Oregon's most profitable exports. By 1893, he had established his own grain business with two separate partners.

His large family emigrated from Germany in 1900 and he and four brothers incorporated as the Albers Brothers Milling Company. The operation milled soft wheat into flour and corn into meal, along with additional by-products. They evolved into the West Coast's leading mill operation with numerous milling outlets and diverse product lines.

In 1911, they completed construction of a six-story brick and concrete reinforced structure following a 1902 fire that had destroyed their main plant in Portland. The imposing building was constructed between Naito Parkway and the Willamette River just north of the Broadway Bridge. The complex combined milling, warehousing, shipping and office space.

When Bernard Albers died in 1908, brother Henry became president and managed the Portland operations. Brothers William, George and Frank took charge of the company's additional mills.

Henry became prominent within Portland society joining many of the city's business and fraternal associations. Under his leadership, the company flourished throughout the 1910s.

His sound judgment then lapsed and he lost everything.

In 1918, he was arrested for drunkenness on a return train back to Portland from California. To compound his misfortune, he belligerently protested his arrest by allegedly serenading the police officers with German tavern songs. He couldn't have chosen a more humorless or unappreciative audience. He was additionally charged with violating the Federal Espionage Act aimed at German-Americans displaying any signs of disloyalty in the midst of World War I.

Henry Albers resigned his presidency in disgrace and spent the remaining years attempting to resurrect his reputation. His legal conviction was eventually overturned, but he was eased out of the company before dying of an abrupt stroke in 1921.

With the emergence of the Great Depression and the decline of the international wheat market, the Albers Brothers merged with Seattle-based Carnation Milk Products. Albers Company became a division of Carnation maintaining their product line name. The remaining brothers were seated on Carnation's board of directors. Nestle purchased the Carnation and Albers brands in 1984. The mill building was rehabilitated during the 1980s and the Albers brand purchased uniquely in 2008 by Continental Mills of Seattle.

Albers Mill Building
1200 NW Naito Parkway, Portland

Multnomah Hotel: An Aerial Experiment For An Opening

Philip Evarts opened the nine-story and 700-room Multnomah Hotel in 1912. Designed by architects Gibson and Cahill in the American Renaissance style, the hotel hosted nobility, dignitaries, celebrities and every American president from Theodore Roosevelt until Richard Nixon before closing in 1963. Between 1965 until 1992, the building housed government offices. Sold and restored in 1995, the 700 rooms were reduced to 276 suites reopening in 1997 as the Embassy Downtown Suites.

The Multnomah earned early notoriety as the residence of Vice Clique Scandal arrestee Horace Tabb almost as soon at it opened. In 1913, new ownership scrapped the hotel's vaudeville shows citing them as *not suitable entertainment for Portland.*

In 1918, weeks after Mayor George Baker took office, the Multnomah was the site of an infamous Oregon Auto Dealers convention. Despite already two years into statewide Prohibition, the riotous festivities prompted a police raid that might have proven a civic embarrassment for the Mayor. Instead, law enforcement officials overlooked the flagrant drinking and arrested a sole individual, performer Blanche Ford for *indecent dancing.*

This incident was one of numerous ethically questionable actions during Baker's extended term at the property. In August 1921, he was photographed in the *Portland Telegram* at a hotel event in the company of numerous high-profile civic and law enforcement leaders standing next to two members of the Ku Klux Klan in full costume regalia. The accompanying headline left the impression the Klan was heavily influencing civic policy.

The opening of the Multnomah featured a dangerous daredevil feat coinciding with the June 1912 Rose Festival. Designed to promote his inventive aeroplane contraption, Silas Christofferson piloted his plane off the roof. The magnitude of the stunt was monumental since air flight was a mere nine years into its infancy.

Christofferson was only 24-years old and his creation was an engineered combination of wood and metal. Called a push biplane, he was obligated to sit towards the front, exposed to the elements with only a single wheel in front of him. He operated two levers beside each shoulder that orchestrated the movements of the plane. An engine roared directly behind his head with a backwards-blowing fan. The entire device weighed an estimated 850 pounds.

Two months prior to his June launch, he had barely survived a Northern California crash. He had lost control due to an unforeseen wind gust and plummeted fifty feet. The plane's front wheel crashed into a muddy marsh causing the plane to flip over and crumple up the frame upon impact. He was ejected from the craft and removed by a friend from the wreckage. He was taken to a nearby hospital nearing death. He miraculously survived his injuries and was flying once again within a month.

Days before his Multnomah Hotel experiment, he navigated his plane from Vancouver, Washington landing on a Portland golf course as a test run. He disassembled the plane and transported it to the hotel where it was hoisted to the roof and reassembled. He then constructed a 170-foot runway out of wooden planks.

On June 25th at 2:00 p.m. Christofferson fired up his engine before an estimated crowd below of 50,000. The plane sputtered, gained momentum and then launched off the edge of the parapet to wild applause. He generated sufficient lift to elevate above buildings to the north and maintained an altitude of 1,500 feet. He flew for twelve anxious minutes before seamlessly landing across the Columbia River into Vancouver.

Christofferson's exploits and daring would continue another four years before an unfortunate piloting error resulted in a fatal crash. He remained conscious as his wife approached the wreckage, but died hours later hospitalized. In 1995, when the Embassy Suites opened, pilot Tom Murphy replicated Christofferson's flight using a similarly designed aircraft.

When originally questioned by a reporter why he would risk death for a simple publicity stunt, Silas Christofferson responded: *This is an age of do it first. Be original; don't copy. When a feat has been once performed the people bore of it and expect the next performer to give something entirely new.*

Although his philosophy prematurely severed his lifespan before the age of thirty, his resolve and ingenuity contributed towards further explorations and flight into the heavens.

Multnomah Hotel (currently Embassy Suites)
319 SW Pine Street, Portland

John Reed: Portland's Disconcerting Literary Lion

Journalist John *Jack* Reed's legacy to history was his firsthand account of the 1917 Bolshevik Revolution from an insider perspective. His book *Ten Days That Shook The World* provided western nations with an insight into the objectives of communism that was also intimately personal.

Reed understood the magnitude and significance of a social class uprising. He hoped that the struggle would eventually become global and the American working class might eventually follow Russia's lead. He was also pragmatic enough to realize such an upheaval might require generations. War has historically been motivated by economics. Reed considered the First World War a conflict between commercial rivals instead of a conflict between idealism. He sensed that capitalism was ultimately doomed due to its excesses.

His conclusions amongst intellectuals and independent philosophers were not unique during his era. Within the United States, such debate and criticism was unwelcome. It became illegal as the nation prepared to enter World War I and later prosecuted under the adopted Sedition Act that forbade all criticism against the government and military.

In current times, Reed's conclusions appear flawed and archaic. The Bolshevik communist party essentially perished during the early 1990s. Collective movements and philosophical ideals however do not always respect history. Idealism may simmer and ferment for decades or even centuries awaiting charismatic personalities, political uprisings and/or reinvention under different names.

Jack Reed evolved into a radical voice. He was reared in comfort and affluence. He was born on October 22, 1887 in his grandparents' Goose Hollow neighborhood mansion located at the entrance of the present Washington Park. His grandfather, Henry Dodge Green founded Portland's first gas and light company and the initial pig iron smelter on the West Coast. Green became the second owner of Portland's water works. He was criticized for acquiring his initial startup capital by *swindling Indian tribes out of precious firs*. Like any frontier era capitalist, professional backgrounds became mucky and muddled with age.

Green represented the Capitalist and Industrialist epitome of what Reed might loathe in his writings. Reed's father married lucratively and was considered an accommodating personality and wit working as a representative for an agricultural machinery manufacturer.

Jack Reed's existence began surrounded by illness, nurses and servants. His life was tracked to follow the ambitions of his family including prep school and graduation from Harvard. He followed those expectations half-heartedly but veered off course upon adulthood.

In 1910, he graduated from Harvard, traveled for six months in Western Europe and then settled into Greenwich Village pursuing his ambitions as a writer. He struggled initially, but his persistence ultimately earned him bylines in prestigious magazine and literary outlets. He cultivated a passionate idealism towards the labor movement, social reform and global revolution. His enthusiasm and charisma made him a popular spokesman and socially desirable.

His most prominent early works included profiles on striking New Jersey mill workers, Pancho Villa's Mexican Uprising, the Ludlow Colorado mining massacre and a watered down interview with President Woodrow Wilson regarding *Insurgent Mexico* that was indifferently received.

Portland had long ago appeared too limiting and provincial. He returned from his East Coast bohemian circle in 1914 to visit his mother and speak at the University Club *against the class system*. He was a rising star amongst political activists gaining much of his reputation by writing for the radical periodical *The Masses*.

It is uncertain when precisely he first encountered Louise Bryant. The most accepted story is that they met during a Christmas 1915 stay with his recently widowed mother. It may have been during a social gathering or a dinner given at his mother's house. Their chemistry detonated and reportedly three days after his return to New York, she impulsively followed him, abandoning her marriage.

Their co-habitation was never conventional and her integration into his lifestyle awkward. He introduced her into a world of intellectual stimuli and notable personalities including Emma Goldberg, Eugene O'Neill and avant-garde actresses, feminists, artistic and literary figures. They professed intellectual, creative and sexual freedom. Bryant initially described their relationship as *so beautiful and so free*! The weight of sustaining such levity proved far more complicated.

Reed was a nomadic journalist and his lack of sexual fidelity proved damaging despite their professed ideals and liberty. The schism resulted in disconnection. Bryant had difficulty finding her literary voice and focus to write. She felt smothered and not taken seriously by the weight of Reed's reputation. They left New York City and rented a summer cottage in Provincetown, Massachusetts with O'Neill. Reed's absence to cover the 1916 Democratic Convention ignited an affair between Bryant and O'Neill.

Reed's return complicated the ménage-a-trois relationship. His need for work and financial sustenance kept him roaming for writing assignments, The relationship between Reed and Bryant took a decidedly convention turn when Reed needed a kidney removed in November 1916. The surgery was considered *gravely serious* and Reed wanted to make Bryant his legal heir. They married three days before his kidney was removed.

They were legally married, but emotionally connected principally by written correspondence. She accepted a reporting assignment in France that withered. He continued a stream of anti-war articles and rhetoric that isolated him from being printed in most publications. His career teetered in ruins and yet his greatest masterpiece was to soon follow.

Louise Bryant accompanied him to Petrograd where the Russian Revolution was nearing its crest. They became the eyes of the West documenting and interpreting the completion of the communist takeover. He interacted directly with leaders Lenin and Trotsky. He promoted their cause through the American media and was willingly exploited as their propaganda tool and messenger.

During the next two years of his life, Jack Reed would absorb several existences of work, conflict and experiences.

Upon his return to the United States and completion of *Ten Days,* he became enmeshed in organizational efforts to expand socialism and develop an American communist party. He eluded arrest and indictment by American authorities through a frantic clandestine escape back to Russia. The Russian border was sealed to outside entry and hostile counter revolutionary forces were still fighting to overthrow the new Communist regime.

Reed slipped into Russia with the intention of returning
back to Bryant a few months later. Permission was denied
for a return by the Russian authorities. He would never
return to the United States.

Jack Reed was no bureaucrat, policy maker or diplomatic.
He was an emotional and passionate orator for a minority
and unpopular cause. He work was a literary streak. He was
honored symbolically but found himself distrusted by many
of his Russian ideological sponsors. He was captured
(possibly trying to escape Russia) by Finnish military
authorities and thrown into prison. He was released via a
Russian prisoner exchange and used by the Bolsheviks as a
propaganda voice and American representative for the
cause.

There was no place in the future of Communism for an
idealistic soul such as Jack Reed. His lack of stability,
imprisonments, beatings and constant agitation aged him
prematurely. The collective dramas, fatigue and separation
from Bryant broke his health. Louise Bryant was
miraculously able to join him in Russia through an
exhaustive and unbelievable journey of her own. He fell ill
on September 25, 1920 while in Moscow. Many assumed
that he had contracted influenza, which decimated more
casualties than the world war. Five days later, he was
diagnosed with spotted typhus and hospitalized. He rapidly
lost the use of the right side of his body and could no
longer speak. Finally reunited with his wife, she could only
futilely hold his hand as he steadily slipped away.

He was in the wrong place to suffer a fatal illness. The
Allied blockades prevented incoming medical supplies. He
was in the perfect location to die a martyr. He expired on
October 17, 1920. The Communists hailed him as a

visionary and hero. They buried him at the Kremlin Wall Necropolis, one of three honored Americans.

Some confidants indicated that during the final year of his life, the Russian Communist Party leadership had disillusioned him. In the United States and especially his Portland hometown, his notoriety was awkwardly acknowledged.

On May 6, 2001, the Oregon Cultural Heritage Commission installed a modest wooden bench and bronze plaque located due east of the notable Lewis and Clark Column in Washington Park. Reed's memorial appears an underwhelming afterthought. The bench directly overlooks his grandfather's former Cedar Hills mansion once situated within five acres. The mansion was demolished and replaced by a condominium complex with a swimming pool.

Jack Reed's *Ten Days That Shook The World* is scarcely referenced today as the Russian Revolution is equally rarely discussed. His name was introduced briefly into mainstream consciousness with the 1981 Academy Award winning film *Reds*. He has become a marginalized contributor within American literature despite the historical significance of his work.

Economic class struggle and division has never been more evident than today. The bubble encompassing wealth, poverty and basic sustenance is bulging. An economic implosion similar to the Great Depression could once again legitimize the prophesy of massive social upheaval.

University Club
1225 SW Sixth Avenue, Portland

Jack Reed's Memorial Park Bench
Located Due East of Lewis and Clark Column
Washington Park
4033 SW Canyon Road, Portland

Former Cedar Hill Mansion
2393 SW Park Place Condominiums, Portland

Louise Bryant: A Companion and Muse With Her Own Legacy

The extended shadow of writer and second husband Jack Reed stretched throughout the professional career and acclaim of journalist and political activist Louise Bryant.

Born Anna Louise Mohan, she began as a young girl employing the surname of her stepfather, Sheridan Bryant. She grew up in rural Nevada and attended the University of Nevada in Reno and University of Oregon, earning a history degree in 1909.

She gravitated to Portland to pursue a journalism career becoming a society editor for the *Spectator* and submitting freelance material for *The Oregonian* newspapers. She moved into the Professional Building as her initial residence before soon meeting and marrying Paul Trullinger, a local dentist who lived on a houseboat at the Oregon Yacht Club. He originally established his practice in suites #809-810 in the Dekum Building before relocating in 1908 to the Corbett Building (since demolished). The couple moved first into northeastern Portland and later the Dunthrope district. She kept the apartment as her personal studio.

Bryant and Trullinger became active locally frequenting and hosting artistic, literary and political events. Bryant was involved with the local women's suffrage movement. She followed the writings of Jack Reed in the national radical magazine *The Masses*. Bryant's comfortable Portland existence radically altered with her introduction to Reed.

He spoke at the University Club in 1914 on the subject of class division. Their initial meeting has been speculated to have either occurred when he visited his mother the following year at an artist reception hosted by Bryant and her husband or a formal dinner hosted by Reed's mother. Their infatuation was mutual and she followed him to Greenwich Village upon his return. Paul Trullinger filed for divorce the following year citing *abandonment.*

In Reed, she found inspiration, encouragement and a mentor for her expanded writing and political aspirations. She labored to establish her own reputation as she found his reputation oppressive to her own. Reed introduced her into the East Coast avant-garde but her own work required years to ferment and deepen.

The couple rented a summer cabin in Provincetown, Massachusetts where she began writing poetry and plays. While Reed was covering the 1916 Democratic Convention, she began an affair with playwright Eugene O'Neill.

Her marriage to Reed was motivated by his emergency kidney removal surgery ensuring that she might have financially security in the event of his death. The couple endured long stretches apart and much of their fragile connection remained by letters. During this period, their marriage and careers were stagnating at a low ebb. Reed became nearly unemployable due to his vehement anti-war writings.

In 1917, Bryant accompanied Reed to Russia to report on the Bolshevist revolution. This pivotal historical event would transform both their professional careers and lives together. Reed published his classic *Ten Days That Shook The World* from the experience. Bryant's work took on a more focused, serious and newsworthy content.

While Reed attempted to politically galvanize American socialists into a cohesive political force. Bryant encouraged public support of the Bolsheviks and wrote of her own experiences in Russia. She defended the revolution in testimony before the U.S. Senate Overman Committee established to investigate communist influence within the United States. She denounced armed American intervention in Russia.

Reed returned to Russia hoping to gain support for American organizing efforts from the communist central committee. His efforts failed and he was requested to remain in the country. He would never return to the United States. Bryant via an improbable journey of her own was able to eventually reunite with Reed shortly before his premature death.

Following his death in 1920, she preserved his collected works and continued her output as a journalist. She wrote for Hearst publications about Russia, Eastern Europe and the Middle East. Her output peaked in 1923 with several of her works compiled under the title *Mirrors of Moscow*.

That same year, she married William C. Bullitt, Jr. and had a daughter named Anne the following year. Bullitt was an American diplomat, journalist, and novelist best known for his mission to negotiate with Vladimir Lenin on behalf of the Paris Peace Conference. Many considered this mission as a missed opportunity to normalize relations with the Bolsheviks after the revolution.

Bryant's health declined from a rare and painful disorder called *adiposis dolorosa*. During the final decade of her life, she wrote and was published infrequently. Her drinking steadily increased and Bullitt divorced her in 1930, gaining sole custody of their daughter.

Bryant gravitated towards happier memories from past visits to Paris, but struggled financially. In 1936, she died in obscurity in Sevres, France at the age of 51 from her degenerative illness. She was buried in the *Cimetiere des Gonards* in Versailles.

Louis Bryant's Apartment
Professional Building
1033 SW Yamhill, Portland

**Louise and Paul Trullinger Residences:
2226 NE Fifty-Third Avenue, Portland**

11801 SW Riverwood Road, Portland

**Paul Trullinger's Original Dental Practice
Dekum Building
519 SW Third Avenue, Portland**

An Iconic Landmark Blemished To Reduce Impulsive Suicides

Towering regally above SW Jefferson Street in the Goose Hollow district, the 120-foot high Vista Bridge is a narrow vehicular and pedestrian span connecting King's Hill and Vista Ridge. The bridge is 248 feet in length.

Constructed in 1926 to replace the former Ford Street Bridge, architect Fred T. Fowler designed the rib-reinforced concrete deck arch. Tanner Creek Canyon passes underneath and the creek waters flow underground, unseen and diverted via storm drains and culverts until the Willamette River. The bridge features 1920s era lampposts and four pedestrian balconies and holding concrete benches.

The bridge has been nicknamed locally *Suicide Bridge* following numerous jumpings, the first occurring five years after its opening. The majority of jumpers have opted to leap onto the Jefferson Street roadway or sidewalk facing picturesque downtown. The alternative perspective faces a MAX Light Rail line station. Following a rash of three suicides within six months during 2013, suicide barriers were erected during the fall.

The fencing has diminished the iconic landmark's aesthetics, but proven effective as a deterrent. Prior to construction, an estimated two people annually died between 2008-2012. Since completion, there have been no reported fatal jumps.

Vista Bridge
1260 SW Vista Avenue, Portland

A Dark Strangler Creeps Into Portland En Route to Further Mayhem

Earle Leonard Nelson began life under undesirable circumstances in 1897. His mother died shortly after his birth and father two years later from the identical syphilis. A fanatically evangelical grandmother raised him. Nelson was expelled from elementary school at seven for exhibiting violent behavior and by eighteen, incarcerated in San Quentin prison for burglary.

Following his release, he was institutionalized in various mental hospitals over the subsequent decade. He exhibited bizarre patterns of maniacal behavior including talking with invisible people, voyeurism and ranting on various apocalyptic themes with biblical fervor. He hallucinated frequently and suffered from paranoid delusions. He earned the nickname *Houdini* amongst hospital employees based on his frequent escapes.

In February 1926, he began a rape and murderous spree that initiated on the West Coast, passing through the Midwest and East Coast before ultimately backtracking and ending in Winnipeg, Canada.

His initial string of five murders stretched from Santa Barbara to San Francisco with Nelson targeting middle-aged boarding house landladies. Eyewitnesses described him as a *dark and stocky man with long arms and large hands*. He was vilified as the *Dark Strangler* and *Gorilla Killer* based on his identified appearance.

In October 1926, he arrived in Portland where he sought temporary lodgings. On October 19th, he raped and strangled 35-year-old landlady Beata Withers and stuffed her body beneath a steamer trunk in the attic of her home.

Police initially regarded her death as a probable suicide. The next day, 59-year old Virginia Grant was murdered and her body hidden behind the basement furnace of a vacant property she owned on East 22nd Street.

Two days later, landlady Mabel Fluke disappeared mysteriously from her residence only to be discovered several days later in her attic strangled by a scarf. One of Nelson's tactics preceding strangulation was to focus each woman's attention on intricate architectural details on the ceiling. By lifting their chin, each victim exposed their throat to Nelson's grasp.

Nelson briefly returned to San Francisco following the three Portland murders. He was responsible for another murder and attempted strangulation of a pregnant woman there before bypassing Portland and staying briefly in Seattle. On November 23rd, he raped and murdered Florence Monks, a wealthy widow and took a few pieces of her valuable jewelry. These items would later confirm another brief stay in a Portland boardinghouse during the Thanksgiving holiday. Curiously an 81-year old man named James Ford walked into Seattle police headquarters three weeks following Monks death and confessed himself as her killer.

Nelson's return to Portland during the Thanksgiving holiday resulted in a boarding house stay with three women lodgers, none of whom he violated or killed. He distributed pieces of Florence Monks' jewelry to two of the female boarders inciting a jealous dispute between them. The disturbance prompted his earlier than planned departure. During his stay, he murdered and raped Blanche Myers in another Portland household He disappeared abruptly with several days of prepaid rent remaining.

A trail of death followed Nelson's eastward movements conducted primarily through hitchhiking and stowing away on trains. Over the course of the subsequent four months, he was responsible for at least a dozen more reported deaths. The number may have been far greater. His legacy identified him as one of the first American sexually motivated serial killers. He disarmed initial suspicions based on his impression of a mild-mannered and charming drifter with unflinching Christian morals.

In Winnipeg, Canada, Nelson's evasion tactics finally failed him. Between June 8 and 10th, Nelson killed his final two victims including the mutilation of a 14 year-old girl. A manhunt for him concentrated on Canadian and American border towns resulting in his arrest on June 16th in Killarney, Manitoba.

He was returned to Winnipeg and prosecuted with swift justice despite being wanted in six American cities and a suspect of interest in additional murder cases. On November 5, 1927, a jury convicted him after forty minutes of deliberation and sentenced him to death.

Nelson's attorneys dredged up an impressive inventory of affidavits seeking clemency from individuals proclaiming Nelson's innocence and integrity. Nelson repeatedly claimed his innocence with impassioned and eloquent pleas.

His final pronouncement was severed short by a hangman's noose at 7:30 a.m. on an auspicious Friday the 13th, January 1928. His final utterance was *I forgive those who have wronged me*.

Paradoxical in life as in resulting death, the hangman's rope proved slightly short for the task. Nelson writhed in agony for fifteen minutes before finally succumbing from strangulation. The ironic significance was unmistakable.

Beata Duhrkoop Withers
Residence: 1933: 2525 SE Lincoln Street

Burial: Wilhelm's Portland Memorial Mausoleum
6705 SE Fourteenth Avenue, Portland

Beata Duhrkoop Withers
Roosevelt A Terrace Section

Mary Blanche Myers
Wilson B Terrace Section

Mable Fluke:
Residence: 7765 SE Twenty-First Avenue

Benevolent and Faithful Ghosts Remain In A Reborn Theatre

On July 17, 1926, the 1,500-seat Hollywood Theatre opened as an ornate companion property to the Liberty Theatre in Astoria. The exterior was designed in the Spanish Colonial Revival style. The interior was modeled after the Roman Baths of Caracalla and the 17th century Italian Basilica of St. Pietro de Lorenzo Bernini. The surrounding district would ultimately bear the name of the prominent theatre.

The two original owners sold the Hollywood Theatre two months after opening and thirty of their portfolio properties to the North American Theatre Corporation. The following year, West Coast Theatres, owned by movie patriarchs Marcus Lowe, Louis Mayer and William Fox purchased the building.

Over successive decades, the Hollywood Theatre hosted first-run films, vaudeville shows, war bond drives, civic events and fashion shows. Theatre attendance followed a steep decline during the 1960s and 70s. In 1975, the Hollywood's balcony was sectioned off and the theatre was divided into three smaller auditoriums.

The fate of the Hollywood was skidding towards the wrecking ball. The original auditorium was left with only 385 seats, many of the decorative walls were painted over, and the original light fixtures, carpets and draperies were removed. A 1997 fire next door nearly destroyed the building. The architectural gem was suffering from a leaking roof, transients camped on the fire escapes and excessive rodent infiltration.

Preservationist repairs and fundraising ultimately restored the building to its former grandeur. The movie palace currently hosts film festivals, comedy shows, lectures, dance recitals and record releases. The changes however haven't reportedly disturbed or dislodged three long-term guests.

The spirit of a man roaming the upstairs lobby area has been frequently observed along with a ghostly woman who sits in the very back row of the theatre. Another apparition is a female spirit pacing up and down the hall smoking a cigarette. She has periodically tapped theatre staff members on the shoulder when nobody is near them.

These faithful residents have experienced the rise, decline and rebirth of a Portland institution upholding the sacred magic of cinematic tradition.

Hollywood Theatre
4122 Sandy Boulevard, Portland

TWISTED TOUR GUIDES.COM

An Early Portland Radio Wildcat Streaks Into Oblivion

Commercial mainstream radio broadcasting has seemingly teetered on its death throes for the past decade. Streaming independent podcast programs appear to be the latest threat to a medium that once dominated American media entertainment. The medium has become niche targeted in much the same manner that cable and on demand programming has fragmented television.

Radio talk show hosts and personalities once outraged listeners with their spewed extreme rhetoric and outrage. Their ranks have thinned and their desperate attempts towards relevancy are now generally ignored.

During the first half of 1930, Robert Gordon Duncan detonated the Portland airwaves with fiery tirades and slanderous accusations. He was a prototype of future *shock jocks* that respected few boundaries or obscenity restraints. His two-hour show was broadcast over Station KVEP (K-Voice of East Portland) on 1500 AM from the Oregonian Building (since demolished). KVEP shared broadcast time on its 1500-kilohertz frequency with several other stations.

Duncan fancied himself *The Oregon Wildcat* and his emergence into the Portland radio was introduced by the financial ravages of the Great Depression. Station owner William Schaeffer began KVEP in 1927, but two years later was losing money rapidly. He desperately transferred ownership and control of the station to Duncan, which he regretted almost immediately.

Duncan ran for the Republican nomination for Congress in 1930 and decided to exploit the radio platform and audience for his campaign. Duncan attacked large chain stores citing their domination over smaller businesses due to their bulk buying and economics of scale. He demanded contributions from local merchants to assist him in his war against the chain operations remaining vague as to his battle strategy. If a merchant's contribution check proved insufficient, he would accuse them over the air of cheating their customers or selling inferior merchandise.

He viciously attacked his Republican primary rival, the incumbent Franklin Korell who won the nomination, but ultimately lost the election to his democratic opponent. Even after his primary defeat, Duncan continued a steady onslaught against Korell labeling him as a homosexual and urging all *natural men* to honor the women in their lives by voting for his opponent.

Duncan's venomous rage and acid tongue might appear tame and almost comical today. As his expanding listenership steamed, fumed but remained glued to his broadcasts, Duncan's rants strayed beyond his allotted time slots. He was uninterested in logic, reason or placating influential personalities. He insulted liberally and indiscriminately.

By mid-1930, local influencers such as the American Legion, Chamber of Commerce and religious organizations united in force to petition the Federal Radio Commission to end the *Wildcat's* siege. Letters and telegrams flooded the FRC matching with intensity and fervor, Duncan's on-air attacks. Portland Judge J.C. Kendall labeled him a *mad dog loose*.

The FRC responding expediently and shut down KVEP's operations. They initiated federal prosecution charges against Duncan. His freakish streak of hot air was concluded but further indignities were forthcoming. While in federal custody, a listener tracked down the 60-year old.

Edgar Piper whose recently deceased father had been insulted by the *Wildcat* slugged Duncan in the mouth stimulating a melee and his own arrest.

Piper was fined a modest $50 by a sympathetic jury. Robert Gordon Duncan earned no such empathy from a jury who convicted him of *indecent broadcasting* and sentenced him to a six-month term in county jail. Upon his release, the declawed Duncan attempted to jumpstart a magazine to a no longer interested audience. He faded into obscurity, finally operating a 9-hole golf course in Troutdale. He died at the age of 73 in 1944 utterly forgotten.

Former Oregonian Building Site (Location of KVEP)
537 SW Sixth Avenue, Portland

A Contract Killing With A Questionable Resolution

On the morning of November 20, 1933, Frank Akin answered a knock on the front door of his apartment. His wife had already left for work and he had unfastened the security chain on the door as he was expecting the arrival of their cleaning lady. Earlier in March, an armed assailant had knocked on his door greeting him with a drawn pistol. Akin was able to punch the man in the face and slam the door on him. This time the armed assailant backed him into his living room with his hands raised. Akin may have been edging towards his loaded handgun on a dresser as the intruder followed him into his apartment.

The assassin almost immediately shot Akin's fatally in the right eye. He may have searched through some of Akin's briefcase papers and taken certain documents. Nothing was specifically reported missing, but there was little doubt that the shooting was a contract killing. The killer vanished within two minutes evading eyewitnesses.

Akin was an auditing accountant who'd just completed an investigation of the Port of Portland and was just beginning one for the Portland Water Bureau. Given the tenor of the lawless times, Akin likely discovered financial irregularities, but were they severe enough to merit his death?

Akin was scheduled to present his findings to the state legislature on the day after his murder. He had reputedly found evidence of the general manager's unethical behavior. The official would be exonerated of all potential charges against him and later became the general manager at the Portland Electric Power Company.

After Akin's murder, his compiled findings reportedly

vanished. Some city-governing individuals had actually viewed the contents stating that no evidence of wrongdoing was discovered. Portland's city auditor George Funk eventually confirmed that conclusion and closed the investigation.

For three years, the murder inquiry stalled and speculation was raised regarding other potential motives. These theories speculated that Akin may have been killed by someone burned in one of his mining deals or by a jealous husband from one of his many reported lovers. His wife affirmed his fidelity publicly, but the rumors remained as glowing embers.

An answer to the enigma emerged from a resulting plea-bargaining deal following a massacre at a beach house in Bremerton, Washington on the Olympic Peninsula. Six wealthy individuals had been tied up and robbed during an apparent break-in. One of the blindfolds may have slipped on one of the victims enabling her to potentially identify the perpetrator(s). All six were brutally murdered to prevent any eyewitnesses.

The follow-up investigation was incompetently managed and miraculously resulted in two arrests. Both men had extended criminal records. One of the suspects traded his *insider* information about Frank Akin's murder for leniency with the Bremerton mass killing. He identified hoodlum Jack Justice as the planner of Akin's killing and Leo Hall as the shooter. Hall coincidentally was his co-conspirator in the Bremerton robbery and killing.

Justice was a low-level Portland mobster notorious for pimping, bootlegging and drug dealing. He claimed to have encountered Akin in 1924 and had invested and lost $300 in a Wyoming *dry* well oil scheme. The consequences seemed too insignificant to merit a contract killing. Regardless, a jury convicted him of first-degree murder and sentenced him to life imprisonment. He would die from a heart attack while driving in southeastern Portland twenty years later.

The alleged shooter Leo Hall was also convicted and hung at the Washington State Penitentiary. His plea-bargaining accomplice only served a short stint in prison.

Portland law enforcement authorities remained skeptical regarding the verdict. Most considered the case unsolved despite a conviction and supposed confession. Jack Justice may have indeed hired the killer, but did the correct source ultimately elude accountability?

Frank Akin Murder Site
(currently Grandview Apartments)
1329 SW Fourteenth Avenue, Apartment #8, Portland

Going Straight: **Portland 1930s Style**

Frank Kodat cultivated a unique reputation for facilitating released convicts desire to *go straight*. Most young convicts went *straight* to his operational warehouse for lodging and to resurrect their prior livelihoods. His warehouse was a complex labyrinth consisting of a saloon, brothel, rooming house and barely utilized machine shop.

His predominantly ex-con tenants were typically burglars specializing in restaurants and drugstores and armed robbers. Their reformation under Kodat's tutelage and protection involved striking targets throughout the region.

Discreetly lodged on the industrial east side, their gang activities generally evaded the overt notice of local law enforcement. Kodat suffered from tuberculosis and arthritis and concentrated his activities on planning crimes and fencing the accompanying stolen goods.

One of his temporary tenants, burglar Jimmy Walker did not accommodate seamlessly into Kodat's reformation agenda. Accused of stealing a wristwatch from one of the other tenants, Kodat decided to evict Walker. Before Walker departed, he scuffled with Kodat and wrestled away his gun. The altercation sent Kodat to his upstairs bed to recuperate. Walker fired a bullet upstairs that lodged next to Kodat's spine. To add insult to injury, he departed the building with Kodat's accommodating girlfriend knowing his own fate was likely sealed towards termination.

Doctors at the Good Samaritan Hospital decided against removing the bullet in Kodat's back due to his fragile health. Walker was basing his discreet escape with Kodat's girlfriend on a drug addict friend's assured arrangements. His allies proved few and unreliable amidst a convict population favorably disposed towards Kodat's interests.

Walker's friend assured him that he could initiate the wheels of immediate relocation the evening following the shooting. In darkness, a large maroon Studebaker sedan arrived in front of the hotel Walker and new girlfriend had hidden out within during the daylight hours. The couple willingly entered the vehicle certain it was providing them an *exit* to Astoria, Oregon.

The sedan, described by numerous witnesses, drove the couple west and was last sighted on a country road near Scappoose in Columbia County. Residents of the farming commune heard gunshots and in the morning discovered the bullet-ravaged bodies of Walker and his female companion.

Twenty-seven people were ultimately detained and interrogated as material witnesses. Both the accused driver, boxer Jack Crim and shooter, Jake Silverman behind the execution were arrested and taken into custody based on eyewitness sightings. The sedan was discovered before the tires had been changed and the tire prints matched those left in the mud at the crime scene. Alibis by both of the accused were flimsy, coupled by damaging evidence discovered in the suspected killers' possession.

The subsequent trial was conducted in Saint Helens in Columbia County near where the murders had occurred. Portland police and the Multnomah County district attorney's office supported the prosecution. Despite the sightings and evidence (dismissed as insignificant by the defense), Jake Silverman was solely convicted of manslaughter and given a three-year prison sentence. He was released in 1936 and returned to Portland to run a tavern featuring prostitution for the next thirteen years before his death from a heart attack.

Frank Kodat survived his bullet wound and returned to operate his speakeasy and burglary ring until 1942. He returned to prison after being convicted of illegal alcohol charges. Doubtlessly, he reunited with several of his former tenants. Kodat's Portland departure cleared the path for another local crime figure *Big Jim* Elkins whose shadow would darken post-war Portland before his self-destruction during the 1950s.

Frank Kodat's Speakeasy Location
75-81 SE Yamhill Street, Portland

Billy's Recollections and *The Guide* Detailing Post Victorian Tainted Ladies Parlors

In 1939, William *Billy* Mayer was a cigar stand proprietor in the lobby of the Davis Building (demolished in 1967). The building was formerly located on the east side of SW Third Avenue between SW Washington and Harvey Milk Streets. Mayer claimed intimate knowledge of stories regarding Portland's turn of the twentieth century illicit history.

Sarah Wrenn had a writing position with the WPA's Federal Writer's Project in March 1939 for the Oregon Folklore Studies program. Mayer seemed an ideal source from which to document an insider's account about the notorious North End of Portland. He had boasted that he had already shared many of his stories with a then famous author, most likely Stewart Holbrook, but seemed reluctant to elaborate with Wrenn.

Instead, he offered her a diminutive booklet called *The Guide: A Description of Amusement Resorts of Portland, Oregon and Vicinity*. This invaluable directory profiled many of the upscale 1894 parlors, nicknamed *resorts* during the era's vernacular of vice. The publication featured advertisements for theatres, pool rooms and restaurants offering private booths for supplementary post-dining services.

Wrenn borrowed Mayer's booklet and hand copied the contents. The following day, she submitted a transcript of her interview with Mayer and the contents to the Federal Writers Project. *The Guide's* descriptive text was composed in flowery rhymed verse celebrating the glories of Venus and her companions for hire.

Mayer credited the composed verse to Sam Simpson, an *old poet of Oregon*. He noted about the proprietors: *they advertised the madams. Yes, they were all called madam then. I don't know why they all have Miss in front of their names.*

Single room cribs accommodating several hundred practitioners predominating the North End *Whitechapel* district. They were operated prominently by French *demoiselles*. Lower Second Street featured Asian and African women. The district north of Ankeny Street was considered perfectly safe for strangers due to constant police surveillance provided a visitor *does not get too familiar with the occupants of the crib*s.

The Guide isolated an area bounded by Ankeny, Fifth, Morrison and Park Streets as a brothel district catering *to a more genteel clientele*. Profiled were several notable parlors that were housed in neighborhood buildings. They included Miss Minnie Reynolds', Miss Fanshaw's, Miss Mabel Montague's, Miss Della Buris', Miss Maude Morrison's and Miss Ida Aurlington's. Today this area forms an important core of the established downtown business district.

These parlor houses would be raided during an 1896 celebrated civic clean-up campaign resulting in no confirmed convictions. The majority of prostitution afterwards consolidated in the North End by the conclusion of the first decade of the new century.

Sarah Wrenn's work regarding Billy Mayer's recollections entitled *Madame's Row* was published anonymously through the Federal Writers Project. During the 1950s, she reportedly worked for the Chamber of Commerce. Her name last appeared in the Portland phone directory in 1960.

Billy Mayer continued his cigar operation in the Davis Building until the early 1940s when he began managing the lunch counter at the Miami Club located at 610 SW Fourth Avenue. His final appearance in the Portland phone directory was 1950.

Portland City Planners razed sections of the downtown's historical structures during massive redevelopment in the 1960s. Billy Mayer's memory and long forgotten passages from the *The Guide* portrayed a forgotten landscape built over with a disingenuous combination of well-intentioned urban renewal and characterless constructions.

Minnie Reynolds' Parlor (demolished and reconstructed as the Lumbermen's/Oregon Trail Building) 333 SW Fifth Avenue, Portland

**Miss Fanshaw's Parlor (demolished and reconstructed
as the Pioneer Park Building)
715 SW Morrison Street, Portland**

Mabel Montague's Mansion (demolished)
404 SW Harvey Milk Street, Portland

Della Buris' Parlor (demolished and currently Morgan Building)
720 SW Washington Street Building, Portland

**Maude Morrison's Parlor (demolished and currently
the Bank of California/Union Bank Tower)
407 SW Broadway Street, Portland**

**Ida Aurlington's Parlor (demolished and reconstructed
as the Pratt Building)
800 SW Washington Street, Portland**

Flora Hoyt's Parlor (demolished and reconstructed as the Yeon Building)
522 SW Fifth Avenue, Portland

The Crystal Hotel: Romanticizing An Infamous Past

The 51-room Crystal Hotel is one of Portland's most distinctive and iconic hospitality properties. Constructed in 1911 as the Hotel Alma on the site of a former logging compound, architect Hans Hanselman designed the structure in the Early Commercial architectural style.

Auto parts resellers employed the ground level during the 1920s as part of the busy West Burnside Street's auto strip. The upper floors accommodated lodgings. The rationing of metals, rubber and vehicle parts during World War II prompted the closure of automobile related services within the building.

The building entered a fresh era during the 1940s as an organized crime nightclub called the *Club Mecca*. Operated by Al Winter, a vice overlord of Portland, the operation became the apex of gambling and rackets within the region. A reform movement in post-war Portland prompted Winter to relocate his empire to Las Vegas opening the Sahara, Lucky Strike and Mint Casinos in conjunction with notorious mobsters Meyer Lansky and Bugsy Siegel.

The space was then occupied as the *Desert Room* and operated by Nate Zeus Zusman. The Desert Room evolved into Portland's crossroads of the world servicing the criminal class alongside law enforcement personnel. The cops kept an eye on the crooks, trawling for tips and inside information. Zusman instituted prostitution services into his existing gambling trade arranging companionship with professionals housed across the street.

The most convenient venues to draw sex workers from were the Georgia Hotel and the Whitney and Gray Building. The Georgia Hotel is a three-level brick exterior building constructed in 1909. The Georgia today remains a stark budget accommodation with Scandals, a gay bar featuring a large exposed patio in the courtyard operating on the ground level. The Whitney and Gray Building was constructed in 1910 and is most famous for Jake's Famous Crawfish restaurant operating on the ground floor level.

Above the Desert Room, a Japanese family managed the *Majestic Hotel*, essentially a drama-free residential establishment between 1946-1962.

Zusman operated slightly beneath the national radar for almost a decade before being summoned in 1957 before a Congressional Committee investigating organized crime and racketeering within Portland. His interrogation prompted his unintended comical admission that he paid off Portland policemen, but considered his payments as *loans*. He confessed that he was an *easy mark* for a hard luck story and added *now they all come around and want to borrow money*.

Humanitarian aid aside, Zusman's influence and operation ultimately receded into oblivion during the early 1960s. The club was renamed the *Red Garter*. Zusman passed away in 1991 witnessing numerous reincarnations of his once fabled hotspot. During the 1960s, the neighborhood changed radically and the affiliated nearby Crystal Ballroom became known as the *Psychedelic Ballroom*. A section of the club space became the *Free People's Touching Company*, a head shop.

By the 1970s, the neighborhood became known for its gay nightlife as part of the *Pink Triangle*. The *Red Garter* was renamed the *Pied Piper* hosting male and female strippers. In 1978, the club catered to an exclusively gay clientele and during the subsequent three decades was reincarnated as

Riddles, *Stark Street Station* and *Flossie's*. The final incarnation was a distinctive sports bar called the Silverado featuring gargantuan video projections of naked men on the walls. The upstairs lodgings were transformed into the popularly frequented *Club Portland*, a gay bathhouse that closed in 2007.

The property's interior was completely redesigned and reopened in 2011 as a distinctive McMenamins' property, accentuated by colorful interiors and decor. In commemoration of its storied past, memorabilia and commissioned themed artwork line the walls. More significantly, the *Zeus Café* restaurant, *Al's Den* (a basement jazz club) and the attached *Ringler's Pub* Annex, honors the namesakes of its former overseers.

Crystal Hotel
1207-1235 West Burnside Street, Portland

Georgia Hotel
308 SW Twelfth Avenue, Portland

Whitney and Gray Building
401 SW Twelfth Avenue, Portland

Vanport's Hasty Construction and Abrupt Demise

Oregon's second largest city during World War II, Vanport was created in the summer of 1942 as a consequence of Kaiser Shipyard's expanded wartime production. Kaiser opened their initial manufacturing facility in 1941 producing *Liberty Ships* to meet an increased demand prompted by the naval war in the North Atlantic,

Following the bombing of Pearl Harbor on December 7, 1941 and America's entry into the conflict, two additional facilities were added in the St. John's and Swan Island districts accentuating a local housing shortage. Kaiser had imported more than 2,500 workers into the region and over 10% were African-Americans.

Affordable and available housing was a perpetual challenge for minorities in Portland since the city's inception. Public housing was dismissed as an unattractive option. Minorities were excluded from desirable neighborhoods by unspoken but understood prohibitions practiced by local realtors. Most were consigned to buying and renting in northeastern Portland neighborhoods, often in crowded and substandard conditions. During the 1930s and 40s, *shantytowns* sprouted nest to the Ross Island Bridge and Sullivan's Gulch. In 1933, approximately 40,000 Oregonians had registered for unemployment relief and thousands lived in *Hoovervilles*, named after the Depression era American president.

Shipping magnate Henry Kaiser fashioned a hasty housing solution with long-term adverse consequences. During the summer of 1942, he purchased 650 acres of land located on the Willamette delta, where the river enters into the Columbia River on the northern periphery outside of Portland.

Kaiser's original aim was to construct six thousand housing units with accompanying infrastructure. His ambition soon expanded into ten thousand units and by August 1942, five thousand workers began laying the foundations for construction. Initially, the town's intended name was *Kaiserville* but was rechristened Vanport as a hybrid between neighboring Vancouver, Washington and Portland.

By December 1942, seven hundred units were completed and occupied. At the peak of wartime production, over 40,000 people inhabited Vanport. The majority were transient laborers with little in common except employment and a bond to contribute towards the war effort. Within the proximity of a single year, the entire community became the country's largest housing project and Oregon's second largest city. Approximately 40% of that population was African-American.

Segregation housing policies still restricted minorities into specific neighborhoods in Vanport and an additionally constructed public housing project called the Guilds Lake Housing. Accompanying street crime and juvenile delinquency was blamed on the African-American influx, but much of the crime was conducted by soldiers and airmen from nearby military bases, the majority of whom were Caucasian.

As World War II scaled down, an exodus of families began estimated at a rate of one hundred per day. At the conclusion of the war, Vanport had lost more than half of its population, despite efforts to encourage relocation by returning veterans. The Vanport Extension Center would be constructed as an institution of higher education and later be renamed Portland State University.

The population decline stabilized by 1948 until the community was abruptly obliterated and abandoned in a single afternoon.

Following two major rainstorms during May and a larger than average seasonal snowmelt, high water levels threatened the levees and lowland construction of Vanport. On Memorial Day, (May 30) 1948, the Portland Housing Authority assured residents that the dikes were safe and sufficient evacuation time if necessary would be available. At 4:05 p.m., a 200-foot section of railroad beams holding back the Columbia River collapsed unleashing a ten-foot wall of water. By nightfall, the city was completely underwater. Fifteen people were killed and over 17,500 inhabitants were left homeless.

The only barrier preventing a worse catastrophe was the numerous sloughs and backwaters in the complex inhibiting the inundation by approximately thirty minutes. This delay provided residents with an opportunity to escape.

The remains of Vanport and the Guild Lake Housing projects were never recessitated. Built as temporary structures with inferior materials, they were not meant for endurance.
The Vanport Extension Center (Portland State) would relocate its campus into downtown. The former residential population eased into the North and Northeastern sections of Portland.

Not everyone was saddened by the development's demise. A National Urban League Director criticized the development as a *nasty, segregated ghetto* and whose destruction ultimately enabled further integration into Portland's previously restricted society.

Several acres of the Vanguard community became the West Delta Park, which is currently utilized as the Portland International Raceway and Heron Lakes Golf Club.

Former City of Vanport
1940 N Victory Boulevard, Portland

1946 Willamette River Floating Torso Murders

The Willamette River's north extremity begins as a southbound tributary of the Colombia River near Blurock Landing and Vancouver Lake. The river descends into downtown Portland severing the city and necessitating ten crossing bridges. Approaching the southern boundary of the city just before the Sellwood district, Ross Island protrudes in the center.

Milwaukie constitutes Portland's southern neighbor straddling Multnomah and Clackamas Counties. Founded in 1847, Milwaukie is known as the *Dogwood City* and promoted to be the birthplace of the Bing cherry. Near the city's Oak Grove district where the Willamette River and Oswego Lake connect via the fingerling Oswego Creek, an unsolved 1946 mystery once dominated the region's media.

On the evening of Friday, April 12, 1946, three individuals strolling the bank of the Willamette River near the Wisdom Island Moorage in Milwaukie sighted a burlap package floating on the rivers surface. Floating debris on the Willamette was not uncommon. The trio speculated oddly that the bundle might be a *bag of drowned kittens*. They diverted the package to shore and made a horrific discovery. When they removed the twine and wire binding they discovered the sack contained the fully clothed torso of a Caucasian woman.

The following day, the torso's arms and legs were discovered at a different river location. The corresponding head would be sighted on October 13th in Milwaukie's Oak Grove sector. Detectives speculated that the packages were originally tossed from the Oak Grove Bridge. The head and limbs had been sawn off and the discarded feedbags had been weighted down with window sash weights. The hands and feet were never recovered.

The victim was described as a female with brownish and grey hair. She was 40-50 years old, approximately 5'2" in height and 125 pounds. The victim's skull was swaddled in a newspaper edition dated from October 1, 1944, adding to the confusion of determining a precise death date. The skull had been fractured leading investigators to conclude that she'd been murdered by blunt force to the head.

The case was pursued by state and regional law enforcement agencies throughout the United States for decades with no solid leads. The victim was never identified and a perpetrator never charged. During the 1950s, the physical evidence entirely disappeared. The river has still betrayed no secrets regarding the dead woman's identity and there is no reason to believe that the case will ever find closure.

Oak Grove Railroad Bridge
811 SE Oak Grove Boulevard, Milwaukie

The Bowden Bomb: A Domestic Fusillade

Pipefitter James Bowden developed an unhealthy obsession towards a developing relationship between his wife Fern and another man. Absent of any tangible proof, he presumed they were having an affair that doomed his marriage. His evidence consisted of observed extended conversations between the pair and her fatigue by his jealousy. She reportedly had asked him for a divorce.

In his version, Bowden plotted an end to his perceived rival by accumulating the ingredients to construct a bomb. He acquired dynamite and detonators, storing the contents in a basement footlocker. He rigged some dynamite in an apple box that he eventually planned to slip deviously into his rival's possession.

His wife and children were aware of his basement tinkering, but completely ignorant behind its lethal intent. He was adamant that none of them should *ever* look inside the footlocker, touch the contents or open a smaller apple box inside.

On July 27, 1946, James Bowden went on a fishing trip. Fern couldn't understand why lately her husband had been acting so strangely. She couldn't fathom what mysterious project captivated his attention so thoroughly. Curiosity prompted her to explore the basement and the forbidden footlocker.

She discovered the rigged apple box inside and instinctively opened it. The ensuing blast immediately killed her and rocked their southeastern Portland residence.

In an instant, James Bowden's obsession for revenge destroyed the singular relationship he'd allegedly hoped to preserve. The only true issue that was never fully resolved was whether the boxed bomb was indeed intended for Fern Bowden or her supposed lover.

He found no understanding or allies at his trial. A jury determined that Fern was the target and convicted him of first-degree murder. He was sentenced to life in prison and ultimately forgotten in ignominy.

Former Bowden Residence
5106 NE 21st Avenue, Portland

The Ultimate Dude Ranch Experience

During early Post-World War II Portland, *redlining* was a prominent restrictive practice employed by banks and realtors to limit African American residents to concentrated clustered neighborhoods. A by-product of overt racism, jazz clubs lined North Williams Avenue and the vicinity. None was more renowned than *The Dude Ranch*.

Owners Sherman Picket and Pat Patterson, nicknamed *Pic and Pat* showcased many of the greatest performers of the era including Lionel Hampton, Art Tatum, Thelonious Monk, Coleman Hawkins and Nat King Cole.

Eccentric décor featured walls with murals of African American cowboys, an ornate ceiling and mirrored dance floor. Waitresses wore cowgirl outfits armed with holsters and cardboard pistols. The crowd accentuated the kitsch with a mesmerizing array of pinstripe and sharkskin suits, neon ties, leopard coats, feathered boas, Panama hats, alligator shoes and Latino zootsuits.

Portland may have been incapable of integrating its neighborhoods, but *The Dude Ranch* featured a multi-racial rainbow of celebrities, politicians, pimps, gangsters and call girls. Diners ate on a balcony with an unparalleled floorshow for viewing captured by roaming photographers.

Accompanying vice related shootings, gambling and the ultimately unforgivable mixing of races on the dance floor closed the club in the late 1940s. An attempted reopening fizzled. The magic had passed.

The building today remains part of the Leftbank Project, a collaboration of community office space, a café and brewery. The subdued stillness seems alien from the heat the space once ignited.

Former Dude Ranch Nightclub
240 N. Broadway Street, Portland

Portland's First and Worst Kept Secret Gay Bar

The Harbor Club was established in 1948 near the waterfront area where U.S. Navy ships docked regularly. Located within the historic Powers Building constructed in 1910, the building has hosted various tenants including a fishmonger, furniture store, cigar shop, florist and subsequent restaurants.

The *Sea Wall Restaurant* opened in 1935, later becoming *Jakes* followed by additional eateries. None became more illustrious or notorious than *The Harbor Club*. In 1948 when it opened, it was cited for an illegal alcohol sale. In 1955, a severe fight occurred between a customer being evicted with the owner and a bartender. The owner was hospitalized from a skull fracture in the aftermath.

In March 1957, the Armed Forces Disciplinary Control Board placed the bar *off limits* to servicemen for matters of *hygiene*. The terminology was code language for acknowledging *The Harbor* was servicing a predominantly gay clientele.

The cocktail lounge featured a darkened mezzanine level conducive to brazen intimacy. During one evening in 1964, officers from the police and fire department cleared the balcony and bar following a city councilman's instigation.

The City of Portland ultimately succeeded in closing down the establishment due to a loophole in the food permit requirements for taverns. Oregon Liquor Control Commission (OLCC) authorities shut down the facility in June 1965. The owner, Johnnie Honegger rapidly reopened operations as *The Riptide* at 949 SW Harvey Milk Street. The city and licensing board continued pressure over food and drink requirements and that facility was closed in 1969.

It reopened again under new management but ceased operations permanently in April 1973.

An amusing anecdote regarding the *Riptide* was a protest movement staged by the Gay Liberation Front against a discriminatory practice imposed against admitting *women wearing pants*. A picket line was instituted outside the bar and soon resolved the issue when owner and picketers negotiated a truce by ceasing the policy.

In February 1979, Paddy's Old Fashioned Bar and Grill opened in the original *Harbor Club* site where it remains today following several ownership changes. Paddy's touts itself as one of Portland's initial *Fern Bars* creating an upscale and relaxed social venue for both men and women.

The Harbor Club (currently Paddy's Bar and Grill)
736 SW First Avenue, Portland

1950 Female Impersonators and Portland's Governing Intolerance

Schneiderman's Music Hall flourished briefly in the late 1940s offering distinctive female impersonators flaunting risqué sexual innuendos. Paul Schneiderman originally opened the nightclub in 1937 borrowing the name and format from traditional English Music Halls. The club initially offered vaudeville style entertainment along with recognized name acts.

Paul's son booked a San Francisco based drag troupe in 1947 that was novel and well received amongst the discreet Portland gay and lesbian community. The performances continued with locally based talent. Many of Portland's local drag entertainers expanded their careers into more renowned venues. Performers were elegantly dressed in extravagant costumes and sang their own songs absent of lip-synching.

The Music Hall parlayed its success with drag queen performances into an extended 1950 run of the popular mainstream trio, the Mills Brothers. The drag shows were included on the performance bill. Paying members of the City Council were mortally offended by the inclusion of female impersonators. Portland's vice squad also attended and provided copious notes for the Mayor and City Council.

On March 17, 1950, Portland first female mayor Dorothy McCullough Lee declared in *The Oregon Journal* that *pansies weren't welcome in Portland*. Lee, nicknamed *Dottie Do Good* had been elected with more than 70% of the vote in 1948 as a reform candidate. Her four-year tenure was generally considered unsuccessful. By the time she left office, she had sent her children out of state and carried a gun for protection due to death threats.

The Music Hall's longevity was numbered. The most practiced manner of closing a nightclub is to attack its ability to serve alcohol. The City Council discovered an opportunity to rescind their liquor license and shut down the operation. Once accomplished in 1950, it was never reopened.

It is difficult to determine how long such an entertainment outlet could have remained under the radar. The city of Portland has cultivated a contemporary perception of lifestyle liberty and tolerance. During the early 1950's, police corruption, gambling and prostitution were acknowledged and commonly overlooked vices. Open sexual preference lifestyles remained clandestine and generally ridiculed publicly.

Portland's broadmindedness would require decades of Post-World War II struggle before it could ultimately claim its *Left Coast* heritage.

Schneiderman's Music Hall
Originally Site: 413 1/2 SW Tenth Avenue, Portland

Under St. Johns Bridge: A Tainted Patch of Forest Brush

In a savage stretch of Cathedral Park underneath the St. Johns Bridge entrance, the screams of 15-year-old Thelma Taylor have been heard to accompany the howling Willamette River gusts. Taylor was a modest and quiet girl who attended nearby Roosevelt High School. She had never dated.

On August 5, 1949, Taylor was waiting for a bus in the St. Johns neighborhood intending to travel to Hillsboro to obtain summer employment picking beans. She carried a lunch pail and a billfold that included her Sunday school attendance record and employment cards for previously completed farm work.

Morris Leland, a 22-year old drifter and ex-convict convinced her to accompany him to desolate Cathedral Park nearby. Leland had known nothing but trouble since his teenage years. He'd been arrested for robbery, auto theft and sexual assault and had been interned in the Oregon State Mental Hospital. He was a savage wolf seeking innocent prey.

Upon their arrival in a secluded stretch, Leland held Taylor captive and reportedly attempted to rape her. His violation was never consummated when he discovered that she was a virgin. The pair reportedly slept that night under St. Johns Bridge, which at the time was shrouded in thick underbrush.

In the morning, Taylor attempted to attract the attention of railway workers by screaming for help. Leland responded by viciously striking her on the head with a steel bar multiple times and stabbing her with a knife. He threw the bar into the river and cleaned up the crime scene. Taylor was buried in a shallow grave under piled driftwood.

Five days later, he was arrested for automobile theft. While in his holding cell, he summoned a police detective in order to confess his role in the murder. He confided that his motive for killing Taylor was *she was a good girl and might tell*.

In October 1949, Leland was charged and convicted of first-degree murder following an unsuccessful insanity plea.

His appeal for a new trial was denied on December 18th and he was originally sentenced to be executed during April 1951. He averted his sentence for 21 months and confessed to a reporter shortly before his death: *It would have been better if they had kept me in the hospital and not turned me loose. That's what I would do if I was running the place.*

Morris Leland was executed in the gas chamber at the Oregon State Penitentiary in January 1953. The dense brush underneath St. Johns Bridge has been cultivated into a closely manicured public park accommodating pedestrians, dog walkers and the spirit of one innocent and victimized teenager.

Thelma Taylor's Murder Site
Cathedral Park underneath the St. John's Bridge
8676 N Crawford Street, Portland

The Deceptive Milquetoast Appearance of A Career Criminal

Frank Oliver Payne masked a vile sociopathic soul with a mild-mannered demeanor and articulateness that had fooled people throughout his life. The 49-year-old bespectacled career criminal killed grocer Hercules Butler during a robbery on Tuesday, January 9, 1951 and compounded the murder by robbing a gas station later that day.

He was apprehended and tried for murder later that year claiming *temporary insanity.* He uttered the classical understatement *I have no more actual knowledge of the death of Mr. Butler than you have.*

Playing possum and milquetoast were classical ploys for Payne whose career dated back to 1920 when he was arrested for a Portland robbery and assault. He escaped from the Oregon State Penitentiary in 1921 and remained at large for one year before being apprehended. Released in 1923, he became a forger in California before being arrested and sentenced to San Quentin Prison. Over the next two decades, he was convicted of robbery and assault in Wyoming, Nevada and Washington.

His criminal track record clearly influenced the jury who condemned him to death for Butler's murder. For two years, he remained on death row and confided to a reporter shortly before his execution: *I'll be dead next Friday and I'll be glad of it. I hope the people of Oregon appreciate it.*

Payne attempted one final deception on Thursday, January 9, 1953. He accumulated a stash of sleeping pills and attempted to overdose the evening before his scheduled death. As with all of his previous exploits, he failed. The prison doctor revived him with injections the next morning and two guards carried him in a groggy state the 100 yards from his cell to the gas chamber only delaying the procedure a half hour.

His execution followed another notorious murderer, Morris Leland who preceded him into the gas chamber two hours before. The grocery store building of Hercules Butler was demolished in 1964 upon the construction of the 405 Stadium Freeway.

Butler's Grocery Store (demolished in 1964)
1338 SW Jefferson, Portland

The Dark Mid-Century Legacy of Crime Boss *Big Jim* Elkins

On the morning of Thursday, October 10, 1968, *Big Jim* Elkins' car veered off an eastern Arizona highway and crashed into a utility pole. An autopsy indicated that his cause of death was massive chest injuries sustained when Elkins collided with the steering wheel.

It was a bizarre conclusion to the unsettling odyssey of Elkins' life. There was no accompanying evidence of a heart attack or foul play. Portland police were suspicious regarding the nature of his death and requested a copy of his autopsy from Globe, Arizona authorities. At the time, Elkins was free on $20,000 bond on indictments charging him with possession of a firearm, conspiracy to commit a felony, possession of dangerous drugs and several counts of receiving and concealing stolen property.

James Elkins was born in Texas in 1901 and dropped out of high school before his first arrest for vagrancy in Salt Lake City at the age of nineteen. His criminal career continued with car theft, burglary and narcotic smuggling before he fired a pistol at a police office during a burglary in 1932. He was sentenced from twenty to thirty years in the Arizona State Penitentiary, but served less than five.

Upon his release, he relocated to Portland where his brother Fred was established operating a brothel and working with a bootlegging gang. Over the next two decades, Elkins would consider himself as one of Portland's *vice czars*, often blurring the distinction between exaggerations with his blatant self-promotion.

His first target became Royden Enloe's slot machine empire. During the 1930s, slot machines were commonly playable in taverns, shops and shoeshine stands. Gangster Al Capone's Chicago based crime network was the major exporting source. Striking ruthlessly during a stretch of Enloe's vulnerably, Elkins and his associates began raiding and confiscating his slot machines effectively taking over his business. Police subsequently raided Elkin's warehouses and seized some machines as stolen property. Elkins' infiltration and reign into vice was merely beginning.

Throughout his Portland tenure, Elkins was arrested frequently but incarcerated rarely. He was rumored to be affiliated with gangster Mickey Cohen and even East Coast syndicates. He recruited a steady stream of young muscle and ex-boxers to assist in his ambitions. He maintained a lifelong addiction to opiates.

In the fall of 1938, Elkins faltered slightly on his strengthening local grip by a federal conviction for moving a large shipment of heroin and morphine from San Francisco to Portland. He served one year in Leavenworth Prison before returning to Portland in 1940. Upon his return, he became more stealth in his activities by paying tribute to local racketeer Al Winter and establishing a network of contacts within city government and the police department.

Elkins had strategically recruited police captain Jim Purcell and others in the vice squad to protect his spreading operations. During Post-World War II, vice, graft and corruption were widespread throughout Portland. Elkins seemed entrenched and untouchable. Pinball machines replaced slot machines. His nightclubs usually operated by his associate outlaws flourished. Anything local and illegal, likely had an entanglement with Elkins.

When reformist mayor Dorothy Lee targeted Elkins for eradication, he remained one step ahead. Elkins promoted and successfully had a cooperative Mike Elliot elected as Sheriff of Multnomah County. Elliot initially made several spectacular raids on local gambling operations that competed with Elkins. The publicity served Elkins well as it removed him from the spotlight. Then Elliot's reputation completely unraveled. It became publicly revealed that he had lied flagrantly regarding his qualifications on his resume. He was then discovered drunk with prostitutes in a Reno hotel room paid for by Elkins. Voters recalled him and Lee's reform movement skidded to a halt. Elliot's replacement was ecstatic to continue *business* relations with Elkins.

Big Jim Elkins controlled Portland, but covetous eyes were being cast in his direction by the American Teamsters Union operations locally and in Seattle. The teamster bosses offered him a partnership package that he wasn't in a position to refuse.

The marriage initially worked for convenience reasons, but soured as the teamsters sought dominant control and a potential replacement for Elkins. Their split was inevitable and soon cascaded into a war of words and intimidation. Elkins wiretapped apartments used by teamster's officials, racketeers and even Multnomah County district attorney William Langley. The parties discussed various crimes and even strategies for eradicating their tiresome partner Elkins. *Big Jim*, sensing his tenuous footing, shared the tapes with the FBI and reporters Wally Turner and William Lambert of *The Oregonian*. The recordings became a featured attraction during the 1957 U.S. Senate McClellan Committee investigation into organized crime headed by Chief Council Robert F. Kennedy.

Eventually over 100 total indictments were handed out to teamsters officials, Seattle racketeers and even Elkins. Following two appeals, he was acquitted of all charges. He had won the battle, but lost the war. The public exposure of his extensive criminal network made continuing operations in the shadows and crevices impossible. As his own stature and influence waned, he departed Portland. He maintained a low public profile until his suspicious death briefly elevated him back into the headlines.

His 8212 Club on North Denver Avenue in the Kenton District is one of the last remaining vestiges of Elkins' former empire. The two-story structure once hosted a bar, gambling den and pinball parlor upstairs and evaded an infamous 1955 raid headed by Multnomah County Sheriff Terry Schrunk. Elkins claimed that he'd given the sheriff a $500 bribe, but during a follow-up trial, a jury acquitted the sheriff. Schrunk later became one of Portland's longest serving mayors.

The former 8212 Club space remains vacant and the legacy of *Big Jim* Elkins is a narrative that has been flushed into the backwater of Portland history. Was Elkins murdered? Motives and suspects were plentiful. Portland investigators were more anxious to confirm his factual demise than determine if suspicious circumstances actually caused it.

Former 8212 Club Location
8212 North Denver Avenue, Portland

Diane Hank: A Babysitter 's Unexplained and Fatal Disappearance

On Wednesday evening, January 6, 1954, 16-year old Diane Hank babysat Wayne and Sherry Fong's young son and daughter. She telephoned her mother crosstown from the Fong's residence indicating they were having a party and planned to have dinner. She also confessed that *she was high*.

Diane was not an average Lincoln High School student. She was blond and nearly six feet tall and had recently borne an infant from her boyfriend.

The next day she went missing. She would not be discovered until more than a month later. Sherry Wong ran a personal ad shortly after she vanished in *The Oregonian* appealing for Diane to make contact with her. The ad remained unanswered.

On February 27, 1954, a road crew outside of Washougal, Washington discovered Hank's body. She'd been wrapped in two blankets that were bound by rope. Her bra had been removed and she had pin curls in her hair.

Wayne and Sherry Fong were arrested for murder even before Hank's body had been discovered. The couple raised suspicion from the outset due to their interracial relationship (she was a Texas-born Caucasian) and Wayne's previous conviction as local drug dealer.

Police investigators honed their interrogations toward Sherry Wong. After Hank's body was discovered, detectives grilled her for sixteen hours, refusing to allow her any rest. The tactic failed. Her defense attorney related a story about a *trusted friend* of hers recruited by the police, drugging her and taking her to a motel. Her friend reportedly attempted to get her to confess as detectives eavesdropped from an adjacent room. The lead police investigator dismissed the claim as *ridiculous*.

The most logical theory emerging behind Hank's death was that she had overdosed at the Fongs' home and the couple crossed the state border to dump the body in panic rather than notify police. This theory seemed plausible given Wayne Fong's criminal background and the couple's presumed certainty that police would never believe an overdose was *accidental*.

For the next four years, the then 23-year old Fongs were tried on a variety of murder counts. During their initial trial, both were convicted of first-degree murder. The presiding judge dismissed the verdict noting that neither *malice* nor *premeditation* was proven.

The couple were tried again, but separately. Wayne Fong was freed by his trial judge due to the flimsy evidence.

Sherry Fong's tribunal ended in a *mistrial*, but her subsequent trial resulted in a second-degree murder conviction. In 1957, the Oregon Supreme Court overturned the conviction and she was acquitted later that year in still another trial.

During the entirety of the legal process, a variety of diverse theories and evidence surfaced. Accusations were introduced that Hank had been murdered because she was *talking too much* about Wayne Fong's drug enterprise. Fong fingered another couple that operated a brothel that paid an odd visit to Hank on the night of her disappearance. Two of Diane's classmates separately confirmed they had spoken to her at a downtown department store on two occasions following her disappearance. Prosecutors dismissed their accounts due to conflicting facts. In Wayne Fong's second trial, two prosecution witnesses claimed that he had threatened them before testifying.

What became certain was that a teenage girl's sudden death left her infant motherless and investigators were exploiting the case to target Wayne Fong's more illicit enterprise.

In 1958, Fong was arrested for dealing heroin. The investigation unearthed one of the West Coast's largest distribution networks. He pled guilty and was sentenced to 20 years in federal prison. Paroled in 1970, he reinstated his drug dealing operations in Chinatown. In 1973, he was convicted of heroin and cocaine possession. He would die in prison three years later from a mysterious fall in the shower.

Sherry Fong remained under the legal radar until 1987 when she was sentenced probation for tampering with drug records. Renamed Sherry Lovell Johnson, she died later that year at the age of 56.

Whatever actually transpired on that fateful Wednesday evening will never adequately be explained. A teenager's interrupted life resulted in an anticlimactic void of unverified suppositions.

Wayne and Sherry Fong's Address
3405 SW Barbour Boulevard, Portland

A Constitutional Argument For The Right To Gather and Drink Openly

The corner of downtown's SW Oak Street and SW Park Avenue was a frequent late 1950s drop-off location for buses carrying soldiers along the West Coast. The adjacent *Tel and Tel Tavern* became a convenient drinking stop and later a popular gay cruising location. The building was originally the waiting room for the Linnton trolley line dating back to the 1930s. The name was derived from the offices of the Pacific Telephone and Telegraph Building located directly across the street.

The Tel and Tel Tavern operated from October 1957 until April 1962. In February 1963, new ownership renamed the location *Derek's Tavern* until 1965, when it became *The Annex* and in 1971, *The Family Zoo*.

In 1964 the Portland vice squad reported that Derek's Tavern was *frequented by homosexuals of higher class and means*. Ballet dancer Rudolph Nureyev and singer Johnny Mathis were identified as prominent clients when performing in the city. Derek's attorney Jim Damis appeared before the Portland City Council in late 1964 to plea for their liquor license. During that era, all gay suspected taverns were habitually considered *disorderly premises*. Damis defended the constitutional right of homosexuals to gather in a public location.

His argument ultimate set an important precedent for future governmental and judicial victories. *The Family Zoo* became a popular gay haven, but also developed a reputation for rampant drug use. The club was immortalized in Edmund White's famous travelogue, *State of Desire: Travels in Gay America*. The non-profit New Avenues for Youth Program offering crisis sheltering for teenage runaways, homeless and former sex traffickers currently utilize the building.

Former Location of Tel and Tel Tavern and Derek's Tavern
(New Avenues For Youth)
820 SW Oak Street, Portland

A Forest Parkland Evolves Into A Murder Playground

On the evening of November 26, 1960, college student Larry Peyton and his girlfriend Beverly Allan drove to Lloyd Center for a shopping excursion. Somewhere between departure and later discovery, Peyton's vehicle became a crime scene.

The following day, Peyton's body was discovered inside his car in a remote stretch of Forest Park. He'd been viciously stabbed 23 times and his skull was crushed. A bullet hole was discovered in his Ford coupe's window. Allan's purse and coat lay inside the car.

Beverly Allan's body eluded discovery until over one month later when a Sunset Highway crew found her partially nude and bound in a ravine approximately thirty miles outside of Portland. She had been raped and then strangled.

Desperate for tangible leads, various individuals were floated as suspects including a career criminal named Edward Wayne Edwards and later northern California's infamous Zodiac killer. A total of 453 suspects were officially considered with only 47 definitively cleared.

In October 1966, one of the lead investigators received a letter detailing events surrounding a large Forest Park house party that occurred on the evening of the murders. The letter implicated brothers Edward and Carl Jorgenson and divulged information consistent with someone intimately familiar with the crime scene.

Indictments followed against the Jorgenson brothers and Robert Brom, a Salem resident parolee who'd attended the party. All three men protested their arrests and pled *not guilty* to charges of murder. The letter writer became the primary eyewitness at their trial and recounted a narrative involving a party beer run, encounter with the murdered couple, drag race, car wreck, follow-up chase and reported *loud crack* that *sounded like a gunshot.*

The testimony proved sufficient to convict Edward Jorgenson of first-degree murder in Allan's death and second-degree murder in Peyton's. Brom was convicted of the first-degree murder of Peyton and Carl Jorgenson was acquitted of all first-degree murder charges. Edward Jorgenson and Brom were sentenced to life imprisonment plus 25 years.

In the spring of 1972, both men filed appeals against their conviction citing the key witness' instability and unreliability. She had reportedly undergone hypnosis and sodium amytal treatments to regain her memory of the events on the night of the murder. The Oregon Supreme Court denied a review of their case.

Edward Jorgenson was paroled after serving only three years in prison and Brom released four years later. Their early release fueled strong suspicions that law enforcement investigators did not believe in their guilt.

If they were indeed guilty, their early release made a mockery of the justice system. If the case against them was essentially flawed, then the responsible killer(s) evaded justice for two gruesome homicides.

Between May 7-June 2, 1999, Forest Park would return to the headlines with the discovery of three nude prostitutes victimized by strangulation. All three corpses were discovered in close proximity and shared a striking physical resemblance.

Police investigators proactively sent out an undercover office that fit the killer's appearance preferences. Rinella Produce employee Todd Alan Reed took the bait and both approached and stalked the decoy on West Burnside Street. Police began surveillance of Reed and obtained a DNA sample saved from a 1992 sexual assault when he tried to strangle a prostitute. Reed was a convicted sex offender who'd served three years for the crime. His DNA matched samples discovered at two of the prostitute murder sites.

He was promptly arrested and pled guilty in February 2001 to the three slayings. He was sentenced to life imprisonment without the possibility of parole. He remains a prime suspect in several other murders including two teenagers slain in Gresham. Both girls were last seen in the company of his ex-wife, strangled and dumped in wooded terrain.

Larry Peyton's Discovery Site
Todd Alan Reed's Murder Victim's Discovery Site
Forest Park, 4099 NW Thurman Street, Portland

Club Continental Baths: A Clean Transition to a Reinventional Use

The Cornelius Hotel was completed in 1908 designed in the Baroque Revival style for Dr. Charles W. Cornelius, Multnomah County's first coroner. His father founded the town of Cornelius west of Portland after emigrating via the Oregon Trail.

Amidst the 1912 Vice Clique Scandal, resident and arrestee Herman Smith inadvertently implicated several men. Smith became aware of an impending police raid intended to round up homosexuals including himself at the Cornelius. Petrified, he fled his room. He left behind numerous incriminating photos and letters that assisted police in identifying men who they subsequently arrested.

During the 1950s, the property transitioned from being a conventional hotel into an apartment hotel. Beginning in the 1960s until the early 80s, the Cornelius housed *The Club Continental Baths*, a popular gay bathhouse. The Club featured erotic black-light drawings on the walls, an orgy room, steam room, Jacuzzi, television lounge and several individual rooms for intimate encounters. Free beer was offered on Friday and Saturday evenings.

The bathhouse became a popular location for community fundraisers and all-male social activities. The proliferation of the AIDS epidemic, accompanying fear and adverse publicity regarding bathhouses during the 1980s decimated the client base prompting the club's closure.

A 1985 fire left the top three floors of the property uninhabitable. By 1992, the property became vacant except for the ground floor. During this period, trespassers and vagrants occupied portions of the building. A 2009 reclamation project was shelved due to the global financial crisis. The owners initiated an application to the city to tear down the structure, but instead the building was adjoined to the adjacent Woodlark Building. It was converted once again into a hotel in December 2018 as part of the Woodlark Hotel.

Cornelius Hotel
(Former Club Continental Baths)
525 SW Park Avenue, Portland

Roma Ollison: One of Portland's Last Gangsters

Roma Ollison was considered by law enforcement agencies as one of the last gangsters presiding over North Portland's gambling houses along North Williams Avenue. During his prime in the late 1950s, he swaggered amidst his kingdom draped in flashy and extravagant clothing. Similar to the emperor without clothing, his reputation flagged over time.

Ollison had been incarcerated for bootlegging and drug trafficking. He operated one of Portland's biggest fencing operations and coordinated robberies throughout the region. By 1970, his edge was rusting. At midnight on February 22, 1970, his residence was dynamited. The blast destroyed his house, car and garage. The bombing represented a serious challenge to his authority status. There was also speculation that he'd initiated the explosion for insurance purposes, He wasn't home at the time. He would upgrade his house with the proceeds finding a property nearby his clubs.

A year and a half later, the challenge to Roma Ollison became intimately personal. Two men knocked on his front door at 1:25 a.m. Ollison answered and immediately began quarreling with the men. They beat him severely before firing a single shot into his chest. While Ollison bled to death in the entryway, the two perpetrators mounted the staircase seeking other valuable items and robbing Ollison's female companion, forty years his junior. They left behind a worn gold plated bracelet with the initials J.W.D. that may have been accidental or a cryptic clue.

Ollison was pronounced dead upon arrival at the hospital. Speculation abounded as to whether it was a rival *hit*, armed robbery, or Portland's law enforcement eradicating one of the city's most infamous criminals permanently. No one has ever been arrested for the crime.

Former Roma Ollison's Residence
2109 NE Romney Avenue, Portland

TWISTED TOUR GUIDES.com

One of the Most Senseless Of Residential Break-Ins and Killings

Colin Hockings, 30 was a married man with two very young children living in an apartment in Gresham. On March 25, 1974, the normally reliable Hockings skipped work. A friend indicated that the two of them had gone to a beer and cannabis party the evening before that had extended into the early hours. The friend indicated that he'd dropped off Hockings at his apartment at 4:30 a.m.

On that same morning at approximately 7:15 a.m., someone via their garage broke into the suburban ranchhouse of Arlene and Howard Weeks. The Weeks took care of two boys, Todd and Kevin Wiebe during the mornings when their nurse mother Eloise worked the early shift at Good Samaritan Hospital.

Wiebe finished her hospital shift and discovered that her sons had not attended school that morning. She knocked on the Weeks' door but there was no answer. Inside she made the horrific discovery of Arlene Weeks in the front room, bound and gagged and Howard in the back bedroom, nude and tied up with an electrical cord. Her sons lay stretched out on the bed and the Weeks' newly adopted four-month-old son Brant was alone in his crib. Each had their skulls shattered by a hammer and left for dead. Only Brant would survive the macabre and unconscionable attack.

Imagine finding your friends and family in such a state? Imagine finding later absolutely no motive for the killings...neither robbery or sexual assault. The Weeks couple was reportedly well liked and respected throughout the neighborhood and their church.

Why the carnage?

Hundreds of tips flooded in to the police accompanied by donated reward monies. A 1965 blue and white Ford had been sighted next to house and a slender man with long curly hair exiting the residence following the murder.

Nine days after the killings, police visited Colin Hockings' residence based on a tip. He expressed no surprise by their visit. He is reported to have responded to investigators: *I wondered when you guys were going to come and see me.* Hockings was an ex-convict who had been coworkers in 1973 with the Weeks at Gresham's state employment office. He lived seven miles from their residence. He spoke highly of Arlene Weeks and denied ever being inside their home or even knowing where they lived. His jet-black hair was fluidly straight and height taller than the descriptions provided regarding the exiting perpetrator.

He was arrested and put on trial for the multiple murders.

If ever a homicide made absolutely no sense, the Weeks' and Wiebe's killings qualified. At his five-day trial, damning witness testimony and Hockings' fingerprints on the bedroom dresser, sealed his fate and sentencing. He was found guilty on four counts of murder on August 22, 1974 and sentenced to four consecutive life terms.

He was retried in June 1976 over the trial judge's technical errors in admitted evidence. His defense lawyers stressed certain discrepancies in the witness testimonies in vain. The retrial jury reconfirmed his guilty verdict.

Colin Joseph Hockings is now 80-years old following nearly 50 years of incarceration. He is interned in the Oregon State Penitentiary. He is no longer lean and his hair has greyed. There are zero prospects that he will ever be released. An alternative suspect has never surfaced in the gruesome killings. There has been no published admission of guilt, remorse or contrition by Hockings.

How does one come to terms with such senseless violence and callous brutality? Eloise Wiebe has been obliged to repeat that question to herself for over four decades. There is no suitable answer in this instance. There is simply sadness and the realization that darkened souls and inhumanity remain among us.

Former Weeks Residence
14019 SE Market Street, Portland

The Recycling of an Immigration Murderer

On December 23, 1976, 74-year-old Veronica Dolan visited her relatives at her sister's nearby house. She strolled the distance back in the frigid evening to her diminutive bungalow. She changed into her nightgown anticipating a fresh Christmas Eve morning.

She wouldn't survive until then.

Sometime during the late evening hours, intruders entered her house, bound her hands and feet together. She was chocked and smothered probably with a pillow and beaten over the head until she expired. She remained dressed in her nightclothes.

The same pair of thieves thoroughly ransacked her house. Their collective efforts resulted in $8 in cash and a medal that once belonged to her sister. Her sister discovered her body on Christmas Eve in the afternoon. The killers were Mexican transients named Juan Aguilar, 22 and Abraham Cruz, 25. Amidst their flurry towards discovery of ill-gotten gains, the pair left behind some tracking clues for police.

They were arrested the following morning. During their spring 1977 trial, Aguilar and Cruz were convicted of murder and sentenced to life in prison. *Life* being a relative term, the pair were deported to Mexico in 1986.

Three years later, Aguilar re-entered the United States as a *conditional resident* after having married an American citizen. In 1992, he was convicted of aggravated battery on a police officer in Altamonte Springs, Florida. He was deported once again two years later. He slipped through the San Ysidro, California border station soon afterwards by convincing an immigration inspector that he was a lawful resident.

In October 1995, he was arrested in Rumford, Maine for drunk driving. He had been working as an apple picker in nearby Turner and operating under three aliases with a pair of social security numbers.

His publicized trail ended on the East Coast, but there is little doubt whatever ultimately resulted in his follow-up 1995 sentencing for immigration violations, he has returned to *El Norte*.

Veronica Dolan's Residence
632 NE Emerson Avenue, Portland

Michele Dee Gate's Doomed Saga That Defies Explanation

The doomed and twisted saga of Michele Dee Gates began when she was eleven years old during the late evening of August 21, 1977. Her step-grandfather fatally shot her 28-year old mother, Diane Gilchrist Gates in the face after surprising her in the act of sex in her bedroom. Diane was living with her mother and stepfather while separated from her husband. Her grandparents raised Michele. Her estranged father James would later resurface into her life tragically. Diane's lover escaped unharmed through a window.

The perpetrator, Norman Reese claimed that he killed Diane because *he feared she'd been drawn into a life of prostitution*. He was convicted of menacing and first-degree manslaughter and served five years in prison.

Michele's cycle of trauma was only beginning.

On November 8, 1978, Michele, while babysitting neighbor *Ruthie* Anne O'Neil and three-year old cousin Nahtyah Ottino, accompanied both to the Washington Zoo. According to her initial published account of events, she lifted Ottino onto a flat board atop a 3 1/2-foot-high fence so that he could view the duck pond better. She then abandoned him to search for O'Neil who had strayed off. When Gates returned, she found her cousin floating motionless in the pond. The truth would later emerge and it would involve O'Neil.

One year later nearing Christmas vacation, Michele Dee Gates would be expelled from the Catlin Gable private school for stealing another student's purse. She would be accused during this same period of breaking into the

O'Neil's house and stealing Ruthie's Christmas presents.

The O'Neil's were planning to move out of state in mid-January. Every parent's nightmare followed when 4-year old Ruthie went missing on January 4, 1980. She was discovered clothed with her underpants and socks missing in a neighborhood backyard rubbish heap. The newspaper account of her death indicated there was no evidence of physical violence or assault. The location was situated directly behind Michele Dee Gates' residence.

The autopsy revealed that Ruthie had been drowned shortly after she had been last sighted. During the evidence discovery process, police investigators detected glaring inconsistencies in 13-year old Michele Gate's statements regarding O'Neil's disappearance. Following an interrogation at the police station, she admitted spending the day with Ruthie. She suggested two separate scenarios prompting Ruthie's death before finally admitting that she had lured Ruthie to her backyard pool with an offer of a new swimsuit and a swimming lesson.

She purposely held Ruthie's face underwater until she drowned in only ten inches of water. She then redressed her and situated the body on the property next door. Continuing, she confirmed that the death of her cousin wasn't an accident. She had intentionally pushed him into the waterfowl pond and watched as he drowned, probably with her forced assistance.

The macabre shock behind a female jaded killer of thirteen created sensationalist headlines. It simultaneously created an unprecedented dilemma. What was to be done with Michele Dee Gates? She was initially moved to a detention facility where she was diagnosed as a *narcissistic sociopath*. She was then transferred to the Élan School in

Maine for three years where school authorities cited her engaging in a *consistent pattern of manipulation.*

For five and a half years, Michele Dee Gates remained in legal status limbo. Her confession was briefly discarded and then reinstated. Finally she was convicted for the murder of Ruthie O'Neil and released into her paternal grandmother's custody. Despite being sentenced to a year at the Hillcrest Youth Correctional Facility (a brief residence of musician Courtney Love), Gates never spent a day incarcerated. She was never tried for the murder of her cousin Nahtyah Ottino. A motive for both killings was never clearly established besides possibly petty jealousy.

Michele Dee Gates slipped into obscurity for five years before returning to headline news in 1990. She filed a petition in Multnomah Court to expunge her juvenile homicide conviction. Despite understandable outrage by Ruthie's mother, an Oregon legal loophole successfully removed her criminal record.

At twenty-five, Gates legally assumed her boyfriend's surname and became Michele Dee Shorthouse. Her boyfriend, Joe Shorthouse had previously been married to a woman named Lisa Mackie. On April 21, 1991, an arson fire destroyed Mackie's Vancouver, Washington house. Following an anonymous telephone tip by one of the participating arsonists to the *Bellingham Herald*, police investigators tracked the source to an ex-boyfriend of Michele Gates-Shorthouse. The friend apparently had received $3,000 of a promised $10,000 to assist in the arson and complete the job by murdering Lisa Mackie.

On June 10, 1992, Michele Dee Shorthouse pleaded guilty to procuring the use of fire to commit arson and traveling in interstate commerce with the intent to commit murder. Joe

Shorthouse was not implicated in the plot. She was sentenced to fifteen years for hiring her hitman.

While incarcerated in a federal institution, Michele Dee Shorthouse remained headline-free. She was released in 2005 and completed her probation in 2008 according to court filings. Her tainted destiny evaporated into yesterday's news while she attempted to reconstruct her life.

Arriving past fifty, she found employment, a partner (Mark Leland) with two young daughters and another surname. Michele Dee Gates became Michele Leland and she settled anonymously into suburban Glendora, California.

The Christmas holiday historically preceded some of the worst calamities in her life. While visiting her estranged father James during the 2018 holiday, her ill fortune victimized her partner. Her father lived sixty miles north of Spokane near Colville.

According to the reporting *Spokane Spokesman-Review*, on December 28th, police arrived to James Gates house to find Mark Leland lying on the floor of the Gates' garage bleeding profusely from two gunshot wounds in his abdomen. While waiting for an ambulance, Leland indicated that Gates was the shooter and he'd given him no cause for the gunfire. Gates companion, Susan Alexander confirmed Gates as the shooter and handed over the murder weapon, a .357 Magnum pistol.

James initially refused to speak with police but when handcuffed and taken away to jail indicated that his motive was *self-defense*. Later than evening, Leland expired in a nearby hospital from his wounds.

Alexander and Gates-Leland apparently did not witness the shooting. Both confirmed that Gates and Leland did not get along. A few years earlier, Leland had beaten up Gates in his California home.

In January 2019, Gates pleaded *not guilty* to second-degree murder charges in Stevens County Court. In October, he pleaded *guilty* to first-degree manslaughter charges. He is currently interned at the Washington Corrections Center in Shelton serving an estimated seven-year sentence for Leland's death.

Murder Site of Diane Gilchrist
216 SE Thirty-Second Avenue, Portland

Murder Site of Ruthie Ann O'Neil
1535 SE Thirty-Fifth Avenue, Portland

A Paperboy Axes His *Rose Lady* Client to Death

Lloyolla Miller lived with her parents most of her life following their arrival in Portland from Michigan as a young girl. Her mother passed away in May 1979 and for only two weeks, Lloyolla lived alone.

She had no children or spouse, but fastidiously cared for the roses and rhododendrons in her garden on the east side of her residence. She was dubbed the *Rose Lady of North Wabash Avenue*. She had been an avid sportswoman throughout her adult life and served in an auxiliary wing of the US Coast Guard.

Her 14-year-old paperboy David Lindell apparently developed a fixation towards the 69-year-old Miller. On May 29, 1979, he savagely bludgeoned Miller in her basement with an ax. There were rumors, but no confirmation of a sexual assault. The murder generated minuscule press coverage, presumably because of his minor status.

He was arrested the following day walking his paper route. He had been sighted near the Miller residence at the approximate time of the murder.

Lindell was convicted of the murder and sent to the MacLaren School for Boys in Woodburn, Oregon until he reached the age of majority. He escaped on numerous occasions and his last published evasion came in September 1985 when he was twenty. There is no record that he was ever apprehended and no mention of any subsequent recorded activity.

Lloyolla Miller's house currently blends seamlessly into

the neighborhood. The once flourishing rose garden is now bare earth.

Former Lloyolla T. Miller Residence
7822 North Wabash Avenue, Portland

Aesthetic Versus Pragmatic Realities Involving Contemporary Architecture

Architect and iconic designer Michael Graves' massive copper Portland Building is currently undergoing a $195 million renovation and reconstruction. Opened in 1982, the 15-story structure features a distinctive variety of surface materials and colors, small windows, and the inclusion of prominent decorative flourishes. It is considered one of the first American *Postmodernist* buildings. Its unique exterior contrasts the predominance of Modernist more mundane steel and glass rectangular and square designs.

The conflict between aesthetics and pragmatism became evident with the Portland Building from its opening. The building is owned by the City of Portland and reportedly leaked from the outset. In a city with Portland's reoccurring rainfall, such a defect becomes catastrophic. City planners determined that renovation was imperative to assure the building's functionality.

Architectural purists have become aghast over the reparative exterior design selected to address the water leaks. Many have threatened to remove the building from the National Register of Historic Places. The exterior will be modified with a fresh façade in a different material from the original. Aluminum over-cladding will completely cover the original painted concrete. Darkly tinted windows will be replaced with clear glass to integrate more natural light into the interior. The original darkened windows contrasted vividly against the cream-colored façade. The change will bleach out the effect.

The covering of character-defining features raises significant form versus function questions. Will the building still be considered Postmodernist with these modifications?

The paradox also raises longevity issues. The traditional rational for employing glass has included economics, ease and speed of installation, and weight factors. Glass is one-twelfth the weight of brick and masonry. Many early styles of late twentieth century glass paneling are only guaranteed 25 years. Their lifespan has effectively expired, but is the cost of immediate replacement justified?

Maintenance and replacement upon deterioration may prove an unforeseen expense making employment less cost effective than traditional sturdier materials. Another consideration may become falling and detached panes, particularly amidst natural disasters. These factors pose an ongoing threat.

Tinted exterior windows created interior unpleasantness in the Portland Building that influenced the popularity of the work environment. The installation of dropped ceilings, a lack of windows and an oversaturation of fluorescent lights stimulated harsh illumination tones. The air quality inside was reportedly bad due to the mechanical systems air-intake vents being hidden on the second level, directly above the automobile choked streets.

The verdict regarding the modifications to Grave's structure is still preliminary and premature.

Early reactions regarding the interior modifications have been notably popular. The replacement clear glass coupled by the removal of the dropped ceilings has radically increased the amount of penetrating natural light.

So how would these changes have suited original architect Michael Graves? In a 2004 interview one year before his death, he offered his assessment of the building's future: *The spandrel (darkened) glass will go away and we'll have clear glass there. So the building will be lighter.* In the same interview, he noted that the painted concrete wasn't his first or even second choice as a design element. A surviving Principal of his architectural firm has given the fresh over-cladding his personal blessing.

Grave's Portland Building may or may not ultimately be de-listed from the Historical Site roster. More importantly, the changes reaffirm that for any classic architecture to endure, flexibility and an organic character must enable design flaw modifications.

TWISTED TOUR GUIDES.com

Portland Building
1120 SW Fifth Avenue, Portland

Mary's Club: Nudity and Legalized Stripping As A Portland Institution

Portland has been credited with featuring more strip clubs per capita than any American city. The reason has frequently been traced to a landmark Oregon Supreme Court decision in 1985 that protected all-nude stripping under the First Amendment of the constitution.

The prelude to the decision began in the 1970s when the Star Theatre showed erotic films, hosted naked dance reviews and upped the ante by bringing strippers on stage to simulate and often conduct *live* sex shows encouraging audience participation. The City of Portland sued the club's owner for violating an obscenity statue, but lost on appeal when the Oregon Supreme Court ruled that *no law shall be placed restraining the free expression of opinion, or restricting the right to speak, write, or print freely on any subject whatever.*

In 1982, an Oregon district judge issued a search warrant for an adult bookstore and the proprietor was charged with disseminating obscene material. He was fined $2,000 and sentenced to sixty days in jail. The American Civil Liberties Union filed an appeal against the conviction and won with the court ruling stating that state law *could not criminalize obscenity or dictate what constitutes socially acceptable forms of expression.* Stripper clubs represented the very public face of a formerly discreet form of entertainment. Mary's Club is considered the oldest and best-known strip club in Portland. In 1954 Roy Keller bought the business from Mary Duerst Hemming, who'd operated *Mary's* as a piano bar starting in the 1930s. Keller employed go-go dancers as entertainment during piano player breaks. Soon the dancers became more popular than the pianists.

Topless dancing with dancers sporting pasties was introduced in 1955. The women performed with comics, singers, musicians and other talent acts. The judicial ruling against Portland's ordinance ban in 1985 immediately introduced all-nude dancing. The most renowned Mary's stripper was rock singer Courtney Love who later performed music at the club after achieving larger public notice and notoriety. Patriarch Roy Keller died in 2006 and his daughter continues the daily operations. The club moved to 503 West Burnside Street in December 2021.

Any shock or controversy regarding stripping or all-nude dancing has long since been neutered in Portland. Tourist guides tout the most prominent and iconic establishments. Most visitors regard the spectacle as harmless entertainment rather than a freedom of speech expression. Neighborhood groups may periodically raise protests over the emergence of fresh strip clubs nearby, but the judicial precedence has firmly established nudity as a Portland institution.

Former Mary's Club Site, 129 SW Broadway Street, Portland

A Fatal Beating Exposes A Sect Espousing Intolerance

Portland's reputation for racial, gender and ethnic tolerance was dealt a serious setback on the early morning of Sunday, November 13, 1988. Twenty-eight year old Ethiopian immigrant and graduate student Mulugeta Seraw returned home from an evening out with friends. Three confirmed racists, Kyle Brewster, Kenneth Mieske and Steven Strasser targeted his car at 1:30 a.m. Seraw and two friends were idling in his vehicle waiting for a parking spot to open up in front of his apartment complex. The intoxicated Skinhead trio hollered at them to move and then savagely attacked.

Seraw struggled with Kyle Brewster attempting to neutralize the violence. Mieske cowardly hit him from behind with a baseball bat and Brewster and Strasser repeatedly kicked him with their steel-toed boots.

Seraw died from his injuries later that evening. The tragedy was reported internationally. The subsequent murder trial unveiled the depth of Portland's Skinhead movement and provocative influence of a West Coast based White Aryan Resistance organization. Brewer, Mieske and Strasser pleaded guilty to attacking Seraw and received sentences ranging from nine years to life imprisonment.

In an October 2018 *Willamette Week* follow-up profile, the fates of each participant were recounted. Brewster completed his sentence in 2002, but was returned to prison six years later following an assault on an Umatilla County police officer. Ken Mieske died remorseless while incarcerated in 2011 of hepatitis C at the age of 45. Steven Strasser completed his sentence in 1999 and vanished afterwards. He reportedly quit his white supremacist affiliation while incarcerated.

The most pronounced consequence following their trial was a wrongful-death suit filed by the Southern Poverty Law Center against White Aryan Resistance founder Tom Metzger. The lawsuit was based on Metzger's hateful message and Portland recruitment tactics that had inspired and incited the killers. In a landmark judgment, Seraw's estate was awarded $12.5 million that effectively bankrupted the neo-Nazi group. Metzger lacked the financial resources to pay the judgment, but forfeited over $100,000 including his house, which was then ironically sold to a Hispanic family.

Metzger was a Grand Wizard of the Ku Klux Klan during the 1970s and over the course of his life has been incarcerated, sued and the subject of numerous disturbing investigative inquiries. Over thirty years have passed since Seraw's death. Metzger's hatred-laced ideology still appeals to an ignorant and racist mindset, even if his own membership base and influence has shriveled. Metzger died on November 4, 2020.

Racial intolerance as evidenced flagrantly during the past decade has far from disappeared.

The Southern Poverty Law Center lawyer who led the civil suit legal battle eventually adopted Henock Seraw, Mulugeta's surviving son. He was living in Ethiopia at the time of his father's death. Henock was able to fulfill in part the dream his father was denied. After completing his education, he became a commercial airline pilot.

Mulugeta Seraw arrived in the United States fleeing a violent civil war in his native country. Violence felled him within his adopted country. A commemorative attachment crowns the street sign at the fatal intersection where Seraw's life was savagely severed. There is no intelligent comprehension behind racism. It remains a cancerous propaganda that ignorance proliferates.

A narrative such as Mulugeta Seraw's should never be forgotten. The vile venom espoused by iconic Tom Metzger figures isn't worth remembering.

**Site of Mulugeta Seraw's Fatal Beating
Corner of SW Thirty-First Avenue and Pine Street,
Portland**

A Counterfeit Ticket Ring and Cadaver Deficient Murder

On January 23, 1990, *The Oregonian* published an article detailing the discovery of 180 counterfeit tickets surfacing for a John Lee Hooker concert staged at the *Starry Night* nightclub. The trail of ticket counterfeiting initially led to a 21-year old promoter from the nightclub named Tim Moreau.

Moreau had taken a leave of absence from Reed College to plunge into the Portland music scene. The *Starry Night* had proven a fertile training ground as the venue was responsible for booking world-renowned musical acts locally.

The evening following publication, Moreau vanished. His last known sighting was being summoned into the owner's office. Police discovered money, checks and related evidence from the counterfeiting ring in Moreau's apartment. His car was left at the airport, but there remained no sign of him. It seemed incredulous that if he had fled Portland, he would have left such incriminating evidence behind.

Later that year a local reporter, Jim Redden began digging further into Moreau's disappearance. His findings implicated the owner of the *Starry Night* in both the felony ticket scam and Moreau's murder. Each aspect appeared directly related to the other.

His reporting detailed the owners' past legal skirmishes and strongly suggested his guilt in the disappearance and murder. The owner filed a $5 million libel suit against the reporter and his newspaper. During the discovery process of the suit, evidence surfaced indicating the owner hadn't filed tax returns for himself or the nightclub.

Homicide is a serious crime that is difficult to substantiate without a victim's body. Tax evasion however is a punishable felony that usually stimulates proactive action by the IRS. The nightclub owner fled to Vietnam where he once again established concert operations. Initially the IRS didn't appear overzealous in their pursuit.

The *Starry Night* was sold in 1991 to a new owner and the name changed to the *Roseland Theatre*.

The murder investigation remained ongoing and eventually bore fruit. The *Starry Night* owner was indicted and extradited. An associate pleaded guilty to the murder stating that he'd held Moreau down while the owner strangled him in a backstage hallway. Their motive was to prevent Moreau from talking about the illicit counterfeit ticketing ring. The associate escorted police investigators to the Columbia Gorge to seek out Moreau's remains. The visit proved unsuccessful and resulted in a plea bargain agreement in 1998.

The owner pleaded *no contest* to murder charges. Both perpetrators served ten years in prison for the killing. One has reportedly relocated to Hawaii and other has remained in the Portland area once again conducting event promotions.

Tim Moreau's body will likely never be recovered. Family, friends and associates remember his abruptly shortened life. His legacy and justice were preserved by an obstinate reporter who despite threats of financial ruin exemplified what freedom of the press legitimately represents.

**The Starry Night Nightclub
(currently The Roseland Theatre)
8 NW Sixth Ave, Portland**

Scott William Cox: Tick, Tick, Ticking...

Scott William Cox was liberated from prison in 2013 following his conviction for the murders of Rheena Ann Brunson, 34 and Victoria Rhone, 32 in 1990 and 1991 respectively. His original 1993 sentencing of 25 years in prison was conducted one year before mandatory sentencing rules would have obliged him to serving twice as long.

Investigators have considered him a *suspect of interest* in as many as twenty or more murders throughout Oregon and Washington. Prior to his 1991 conviction, he was a long haul trucker enabling him to travel freely interstate throughout the country. One disturbing suspected murder included the April 1991 grisly discovery of prostitute Tia Hicks' body in a boat parked outside of a Mountlake Terrace, Washington bingo hall.

Since 1975, Cox has been admitted to mental institutions 115 times. He has been convicted of forgery and gun theft and acknowledged cocaine use and violence against women.

Since his prison release, lifetime parole, and designation as a sex offender, he is obligated to wear a GPS tracking device and reportedly geographically restricted to Yamhill County. He is required to avoid parks, bars, children and schools. He has been arrested at least six times for parole violations, although details have not been provided to the public.

Cox's circumstances have become a clear example of a parolee's rights versus endangerment to the general pubic. Is he indeed a reformed serial killer? Can one exist?

**Rheena Ann Brunson's Discovery Site
Safeway Store Parking Lot
5920 NE Martin Luther King Boulevard, Portland**

**Victoria Rhone's Discovery Site
Train car in Portland rail yard**

Confessional Controversy Over a Potential Prostitute Serial Killer

Over the course of three decades, five prostitutes in North Portland were discovered slain by strangulation. Each worked along Martin Luther King Jr. Boulevard (formerly known as Union Avenue). Law enforcement investigators noticed similarities in the crimes including each woman was sexually assaulted with their shirts pushed over their chest. A common male DNA profile was discovered on each victim. Four of the five bodies were deposited within a one-mile radius.

In October 2015, police arrested a suspect, Homer Lee Jackson who has remained in custody since. He was accused of killing Tonja Harry, 19, in July 1983, Angela Anderson, 14, in September 1983 and Latanga Watts, 29, in March 1987. He was later charged with the murder of Essie Jackson killed in March 1983, but the charges were later dismissed. Jackson remains a prime suspect.

What essentially appeared a solid case against a sexual serial killer began to teeter in 2017 when a Multnomah County Circuit Judge threw out confessionary statements made by Jackson to two Portland cold case detectives while in custody. The judge ruled that during more than seven hours of questioning extended over two days, Jackson's statements were *made under the influence of fear produced by threats (and promises of leniency)*.

The court determined that the detectives' methods and inducements might have prompted Jackson to confess to them what they wanted to hear regardless of whether it was true. It further noted Jackson's diagnosed schizophrenia and memory loss often revealed incorrect details about some of the killings.

The court reportedly found disturbing the detectives' suggestion that if Jackson didn't confess, he might be tied to additional murders or crimes. The result would be a jury considering him a *monster* and recommending him the maximum possible sentence. In December 2018, the Oregon Supreme Court upheld the lower court's ruling leaving Jackson's fate in virtual limbo.

Whoever was directly responsible for the four murders is unquestionably a *monster* and evidence coupled by Jackson's documented statements make him the most likely candidate. The tactics employed by the investigating detectives raise the elemental question as to the extent police may employ to obtain relevant information. In Jackson's example, there was nothing published that he had an attorney present during questioning preventing him from self-incrimination.

On May 28, 2019, prosecutors added an additional indictment against Jackson for the 1993 killing of Lawauna Janelle Triplet, 29. The murder followed a similar pattern as the other four women. The new charges raised the total to fifteen counts of aggravated murder stemming from the four deaths. Jackson's trial is set for 2020.

Ethical questions have been raised, but even more pertinent is whether a North Portland serial killer is responsible for even more deaths. Regardless of one's personal opinion regarding the occupation, streetwalking sex workers are amongst the most vulnerable and preyed upon women in society.

At least four deaths may one day be tied directly to a convicted perpetrator.

Tonya Harry's Body Discovery
Slough Bordering West Delta Park (between Portland
International Raceway and Heron Lakes Golf Club

Essie Jackson's Body Discovery
Overlook Park, Portland

**Angela Anderson's Body Discovery
400 Block of NE Going Street, Portland**

**Latanga Watts' Body Discovery
Empty Lot: North Concord Avenue & North Going Ct.**

**Lawauna Triplet's Body Discovery
Pedestrian Overpass, North Going Street and Concord
Avenue, Portland**

A Seemingly *Regular Guy* Bloodies Portland's Night Scene

Erik Salvador Ayala by the age of 24 had a reputation for timidity and simply blending in. On January 9, 2009, he entered a Portland pawnshop and purchased an Italian-made Tanfoglio 9mm semiautomatic pistol. He didn't appear to be an experienced gun owner and asked about learning to shoot. The pawnshop owner recommended a gun safety course.

He noted that Ayala was *polite, he was friendly, he seemed like a regular guy.*

Neighbors in his suburban Milwaukie apartment complex observed that Ayala was a quiet and friendly resident in an area riddled with crime. The apartment manager lived across from Ayala and noted the two had previously traded small talk, with video games a primary topic. Ayala paid his rent promptly and never spoke of any financial troubles or other problems. The manager had once entered Ayala's apartment for repairs and observed *it appeared especially clean. Nothing about the apartment seemed particularly out of the ordinary.*

The manager observed Ayala *was always really calm-didn't seem really too up or down.*

Ayala worked for the Oregon Department of Human Services in Salem as a data entry clerk during 2006 and 2007. He reportedly worked through temporary employment agencies afterwards. He had been unemployed for a period leading up to the January 2009.

Those closest to him reported that Ayala *did not frequent dance clubs, was not a violent person, nor ever exhibited an interest in firearms. He enjoyed playing video games focused on battling alien races and zombie attacks.*

The Zone was a well-established predominantly under 21 dance club that didn't serve alcohol. On Saturday evening January 24, 2009, eleven foreign exchange students were attending a Rotary International Youth social outing organized by a parent to celebrate a Guatemalan student's birthday. *The Zone* seemed an ideal downtown location and safe environment.

At approximately 10:30 p.m. that evening, Erik Ayala parked his car a few blocks away and strolled towards the nightclub. His choice was likely arbitrary as he suddenly began firing indiscriminately. The foreign exchange teenagers and customers waiting outside the entrance to Kell's Irish Pub next door were in the line of fire. He knew none of his targets personally and did not enter either building.

His shots almost instantly killed 16-year-old Ashley Lauren Wilks and 17-year-old Martha Paz De Noboa. He wounded seven others including the general manager of Kell's. Following the fusillade, Ayala raised the gun to his head and pulled the trigger. He died the following Tuesday afternoon at Legacy Emanuel Hospital.

The abruptness and shock from the killings triggered questions into an apparent motive. Investigators discovered that Ayala had been diagnosed as a schizophrenic during high school. He had once attempted suicide with over-the-counter drugs. While working at a Burger King, he threw his prescribed medication into the garbage. Ultimately, an explainable motive never emerged except that his rampage-suicide was premeditated.

Ayala left a note in his apartment. It read:

To my friends and family:
I am sorry.

And to my friend (his roommate)
I am especially sorry. I know it's not much consolation but as my friend and roommate you are entitled to everything that I own. Maybe these things can bring in a few bucks.

The note detailed information regarding his financial accounts, alien resident number, car and ps3 video game system. He ironically noted a leaking oil problem with the vehicle. He suggested asking prices for each of his potential resale items.

He closed the note with *I'm sorry to put all this on you buddy, good luck.*

The Zone never recovered its core business following the notoriety. It shuttered permanently in April 2009. The building is currently operating as the Pine Street Market.

Erik Salvador Ayala had attempted to reconcile orderly closure with his own life. Yet he was callously unmindful of the tragedy and chaos he was prepared to inflict on others.

**The Zone Nightclub (currently Pine Street Market)
126 SW Second Avenue, Portland**

Family Values and A Corrupting Community Influence

Yam Yam's Southern Barbeque suffered a decline in the caliber of their restaurant reviews around 2007. The restaurant's modest North Portland location and neighborhood had always been considered a liability to fine dining, but the quality of their food appeared sound.

In late October 2009, the perception of Yam Yam's altered significantly when one of their *cooks*, James *Lonnie* Yoakum was arrested for operating a $300,000 a month cocaine operation. Yam Yam's was reportedly used as a front to launder funds and create the appearance of a legitimate business.

Police had suspected Yoakum as a drug distributor for decades, but never had sufficient evidence to arrest and convict him. Employing wiretaps and various surveillance tactics, police arrested Yoakum carrying $11,000 in cash and more than $60,000 in the restaurant safe. Law enforcement authorities indicated that Yoakum distributed cocaine powder and crack crystal via Crip gang members.

Yoakum's arrest was hastened by a nearby shooting in late August 2009. Detectives were already tapping his cell phone when they intercepted a conversation from his son asking for his assistance in the aftermath. His son had reportedly shot a rival gang member. Lonnie Yoakum agreed to pick up his son and drive him out of state. His son was arrested in Seattle and charged with assault, unlawful use of a firearm and attempted murder.

The phone taps over an eighth month period allowed police to track the drug dealers' movements. Messages by the perpetrators were coded in golf vernacular. Yoakum, his son and another participant were arrested the same weekend as 21 other individuals as part of a multi-agency Metro Gang Task Force sting.

Yam Yam's owner and head chef was never charged with drug trafficking. Federal officials investigated him on charges of money laundering, but charges were never publicly reported. Despite the excessive amount of cash discovered in his restaurant safe, he owed approximately $425,000 in bank debt on the property. Paying his mortgage was apparently not a priority. His building was put up for auction in June 2010 and operation closed immediately upon Yoakum's arrest.

Lonnie Yoakum was sentenced to thirteen years in prison for drug distribution. Two of his sons were subsequently arrested in later shooting incidents. The depressing scenario behind this criminal family sharing incarceration as a core value is tragic. Worse, it has become a frequent occurrence amongst contemporary prison populations.

Former Yam Yam's Restaurant Site
7339 NE Martin Luther King Jr. Blvd, Portland

A Questionable Medical Determination Potentially Clouds A Murder Investigation

Fifty-seven-year old Oregon Assistant Federal Public defender Nancy Bergeson was a formidable courtroom presence described as *relentless* and *a really good lawyer* by her peers and professional adversaries. She had a robust personality and was extremely physically fit. She traveled extensively, was an avid paddle boarder, climbed mountains, skied and ran marathons.

Her residence was located in a middle-class southwestern Portland neighborhood. Her front and backyard was surrounded by a white picket fence (the fence has since been replaced). Her comfortable oasis from occupational stressors was decorated with artifacts from her travels. In such a perceptively secure environment, peril seemed impregnable. This reality proved illusionary.

On Tuesday afternoon, November 24, 2009 at 3 p.m., a neighborhood girl who'd stopped by to walk Bergeson's golden retriever viewed her body through a front window. She was sprawled on her dining room floor. The girl alerted a neighbor who called the police. Patrol officers arrived at Bergeson's home along with a forensic criminologist and deputy medical examiner.

The deputy medical examiner concluded that her death was by *natural causes* and the body was subsequently moved. Based on this presumption, police investigators may not have exercised the identical prudence as a procedural crime scene. Potential key evidence may have been compromised.

Following the completion of an autopsy the next morning, the conducting state medical examiner found internal neck injuries consistent with strangulation and petechiae hemorrhages (tiny red spots caused by broken capillaries).

Law enforcement authorities began backpedaling on their inadvertent breach of protocol in investigating a potential crime scene.

The state medical examiner that conducted the autopsy publicly was quoted in her belief that the scene was secured and no evidence lost during the 16 hours between when the body was discovered and autopsy conducted. She noted that the *criminalist took a lot photos and the house was secured and locked*. Upon returning the next day, nothing had visually been disturbed.

One of Bergeson's professional peers, a Portland defense attorney was less certain. Quoted regarding the investigators, she observed: *They just tramped around. Who knows what trace evidence was there that's gone now?*

The senior medical examiner that conducted the autopsy publicly softened judgment on her colleague's erroneous conclusion by stating petechiae hemorrhages are not specific to strangulation. She noted *they were often seen in living people, not always visible in non-clinical settings and strangulations done with broad, soft cloths do not leave outside appearances.*

Bergeson's murder investigation stalled for nearly a decade. The controversy surrounding the crime scene investigation and potentially lost evidence did not recede. One of the puzzling dilemmas was how an extremely fit and forceful woman could have been simply overpowered with minimal trace. Police confirmed later that they'd found evidence that she had fought with her attacker. This conclusion seemed contradictory in light of the deputy medical examiner's original *death by natural causes* conclusion. How could such overt evidence be overlooked?

During the decade the case seemed suspended in inertia, two probable theories were discounted. A professional hit or killing related to her work as a criminal defense lawyer were essential dismissed.

In December 2016, investigators received a break resulting in an arrest when an eyewitness to the murder spoke indiscreetly. Justin Joseph Panek bragged to another wiretapped inmate while incarcerated on an unrelated robbery charge about his presence at the killing. Panek indicated that Bergeson was his grandfather's neighbor and he used to cut through her yard frequently with her door often left open. During the Thanksgiving 2009 holiday while visiting his grandfather, he and a friend, Christopher Alexander Williamson saw her door open and no sign of her vehicle parked outside.

The pair entered and Panek began rummaging through her belongings downstairs. Bergeson was apparently home and suddenly appeared surveying their burglary in process. Williamson locked her in a chokehold that apparently strangled her.

According to Panek, both men had been questioned previously by Portland detectives but were not charged then. Both admitted to breaking into the house, but claimed it was on another occasion.

Christopher Alexander Williamson was arrested on January 19, 2019 at a dialysis clinic in Tualatin. He underwent treatment there three times weekly for kidney ailments.

Williamson's reported past had included convictions for being a minor in possession of alcohol and a third-degree assault charge. He had been arrested previously for assaulting his father, but the charge was later dropped following his completion of a diversion program. His father had a history of convictions for sex crimes. At the time of the killing, Williamson reportedly lived nearby Bergeson's residence.

Williamson would be arraigned the following week and initially pleaded *not guilty* to murder charges. In March 2020, he revised his plea to guilty and was sentenced to 15 years imprisonment. He is currently incarcerated at Two Rivers Correctional Institution in Umatilla. Panek was convicted of first-degree burglary in September 2017 and served his sentence at Two Rivers Correctional Institution.

Nancy Bergeson's Residence
4146 SW Hamilton Street, Portland

Kyron Horman: A Child Abduction Scheduled Between a Science Fair and First Period

Skyline Elementary School bears no resemblance to any other school within the Portland school district. Located on an isolated hilltop road in the far northwestern quarter of Forest Park, the neighborhood is rural, wooded and a steep ascent above Highway 30 that traces the Willamette River. It would appear superficially an unlikely location for child abduction.

On June 4, 2010, 7-year old Kyron Horman attended a science fair at the school and posed for a photograph at the event. His stepmother reportedly last sighted him at approximately 8:45 a.m. walking down the hall towards his first class. He was never seen in that first class or the rest of the school day. He was not reported missing until he failed to return home in the afternoon on the school bus.

Search efforts began immediately afterwards within a 2-mile radius around the school and the nearby Sauvie Island Bridge. Over the subsequent ten days, hundreds of volunteer and trained rescuers kept up the search and escalating rewards were offered.

The same months as Kyron's disappearance, suspicion was cast on the stepmother who failed two separate polygraph examinations regarding Kyron's disappearance. A story also circulated that she had offered their landscape gardener money previously to kill her husband. The charge could not be proven, but Kyron's father filed for divorce by the end of the month and obtained a restraining order against her

In 2012, Kyron's birth mother filed a civil lawsuit against the stepmother claiming responsibility for Kyron's disappearance. A year later, the lawsuit was withdrawn. The stepmother has appeared on the *Dr. Phil* television show claiming her innocence. The law enforcement investigation remains ongoing but increasingly frigid.

There still remains no trace of Kyron Horman and the search continues for a body that may never be retrieved or a kidnapping with no confirmed responsible party.

Skyline Elementary School
11536 NW Skyline Blvd. Portland

Brittany Maynard: A Solitary Ripple Fuels An Ocean of Discussion

At the age of twenty-nine, Brittany Maynard relocated to Portland from her native California to savor her final home, happiness and breath. Her upbringing in Orange County was followed by university degrees from UC Berkeley and the University of California, Irvine. She traveled extensively and had taught in orphanages in Nepal. She married in September 2012 and planned to start a family with her husband.

An unanticipated medical diagnosis intervened a little over a year later.

In early 2014, she was diagnosed with brain cancer and following a cranial operation, the cancer returned and her prognosis was elevated to terminal. She was given a prognosis of six months to live.

The state's *Death with Dignity Law* that legalized assisted suicide prompted her relocation to Oregon as her final destination. In 2014, Oregon was one of three states that permitted legalized assisted death.

Maynard generated international attention for her activism in the death with dignity movement and for the legalization of assisted death. As an attractive and vivacious young woman, her example became the antithesis of the average patient seeking physician-assisted death. The average age for participants was 71-years old in Oregon.

In seeking to terminate her life legally on her terms, she stirred up controversy from a variety of organizations ranging from the Vatican to several terminally ill individuals. Despite the polarized opinions, debate on assisted suicide was elevated from its former taboo status into public discussion via the news media.

On November 1, 2014 surrounded by her family and those closest to her, she slipped silently into death with drugs prescribed by her doctor. Her final posted writing succinctly summarized her epitaph: *Goodbye to all my dear friends and family that I love. Today is the day I have chosen to pass away with dignity in the face of my terminal illness...this terrible brain cancer that has taken so much from me...but would have taken so much more.*

Six dditional states have since legalized medically assisted suicide since Maynard's passing. Similarly themed legislation continues to be introduced and subsequently challenged in court. Death remains an uncomfortable subject. One courageous woman ignored the world's scrutiny and even condemnation to assert control of her unique destiny.

Brittany Maynard Suicide Location
3108 NW Verde Vista Terrace, Portland

A Double Life Terminated Violently on a Hotel Stairwell

Ashley Benson lived a double life attempting to straddle the demands of being a responsible single mother and earning an income as an escort and prostitute. Her life ended abruptly sprawled inside the eighth floor stairwell of Portland's Doubletree Hotel on December 26, 2014. An employee of the hotel discovered her strangled with no explanation of how her body ended up there or why she was even at the property as an unregistered guest.

As the investigation into her death deepened, the name of Chris Youn emerged as a possible suspect. He had checked into the hotel Christmas Day, 24 hours earlier than his scheduled reservation. Searching his room, police discovered one of Benson's fingernails and a telephone log of calls made from the room to a number featured on an escort advertisement on a website called BackPage.com. The ad promoted the dead woman's sexual services and availability.

The actual Chris Youn innocently checked into the hotel on December 26th shocking police. The confusion was sorted out when it was discovered another man had assumed his identity and referenced his reservation the day before. His name was Chris Yoon (spelled slightly differently). Both resided in the same complex in Bellevue, Washington.

The fragments behind Benson's encounter with Yoon began to piece together. One of her acquaintances presumed to be her boyfriend was actually her pimp. He admitted to dropping Benson off at the Doubletree on the day of the murder for a scheduled sexual encounter. Police obtained a warrant to track suspect Chris Yoon's cell phone and the initial ping hits traced him to Portland and another hotel.

Two weeks following Ashley Benson's murder, he would be arrested at Portland's Union Station incredulously asking officers: *How did you find me?*

Law enforcement surveillance has become more sophisticated over time. Violence against sex workers remains a historical and ongoing danger. Benson's family professed complete ignorance regarding her dual life and filed a $3.6 million lawsuit against Backpage.com and the Hilton Hotel chain (owners of Doubletree) citing *both businesses failed to establish and use practices to protect victims of sex trafficking*.

Ironically, eleven months before her murder, a Multnomah County judge reportedly had warned her about the dangers of her escort work and removed her young son from her custody.

The motive behind Benson's killing was ultimately publicized as either a dispute over payment and/or Yoon's possessiveness and attempt to coerce her out of escort work to become his steady boyfriend.

In June 2017, Yoon was found guilty of first-degree murder and sentenced to 18 years in prison. He is currently interned at the Oregon State Correctional Institution in Salem following a stint at the Eastern Oregon Correctional Institute in Pendleton.

TWISTED TOUR GUIDES.com

Doubletree Hotel
1000 NE Multnomah Street, Portland

Murder Site: Eighth Floor Stairwell

Hotel Joyce: Outlet Rebirth For A Desperate Segment of Society

The Hotel Joyce building represents a challenge every major American urban center faces addressing chronic homelessness and the dire need for affordable housing or inexpensive traveler accommodations. The Joyce became Portland's last single-room occupancy hotel before being purchased by the City's Housing Bureau for $4.22 million in 2016. Prior to the purchase, the property was considered *last resort housing*. The purchase was part of city official's promise to preserve affordable rental units downtown.

The Joyce was constructed in 1912 and previously operated as the budget Hotel Treves. Beginning in 1965, the owner offered furnished rooms for longer-term and government assisted clientele. Periodically travelers booked overnight accommodations. Many were rumored to be newly released prisoners experiencing initial freedom following incarceration. Most of the long-term lodgers preferred the hotel as an alternative to homeless shelter facilities due to the improved hygiene and privacy.

The Joyce's history was not entirely drama free. Several residents died from overindulgence from drugs and alcohol combined with periodic falls down the main staircase. In 1991, a man fell to his death after attempting to rappel from a hotel window using a bedsheet. The same year, a guest stabbed another in the heart and in 2010, a strangulation murder was recorded.

During the 2016 eviction process, approximately 90 permanent residents were transferred to alternative living locations. The process of relocation was often slow and laborious. One wheelchair bound woman who habitually crawled up a flight of stairs to her room each night had to be hand carried down to a transfer van. A rent assistance grant from the Portland Housing Bureau assisted many tenants to find housing and pay their deposits and first month's rent.

The hotel re-opened as *The Joyce* in Spring 2023 providing 66 units for people exiting homelessness. The additional bed capacity will assist but have minimal impact on Portland's impoverished and destitute population.

Homelessness has evolved into a global urban challenge that offers few if any promising solutions.

Hotel Joyce
322 SW Eleventh Avenue, Portland

Gordon Sondland: 48 Hours of Global Scrutiny

For 48 hours during the Trump impeachment hearings in November 2019, Gordon Sondland became exposed to international consciousness. The appointed U.S. Ambassador to the European Union implicated Trump and the leadership of the State Department and National Security Council regarding their complicity in a policy demand to the Ukraine. In exchange for continued American financial support, the Ukraine government was requested to announce a criminal investigation into the Biden family, a political opponent of Trump, for activities in their country. In his diplomatic role, Sondland was considered the communications channel between the Trump administration and Ukrainian officials.

Many supporters of Trump and the Republican Party who had downplayed the extent and significance of this request perceived Sondland's testimony as a betrayal. His testimony before the U.S. Senate and television audiences dramatically raised the profile of a previously obscure Portland hotelier.

Sondland was raised in Mercer Island, Washington and attended the University of Washington before dropping out and becoming a commercial real state salesman. His company, Provenance Hotels, owns and operates fourteen properties throughout the United States with six in Portland. His Portland hotels include the Hotel deLuxe, Hotel Lucia, Sentinel Hotel, Heathman Hotel, Hotel Dossier and the Woodlark Hotel. The company is known for designing or remodeling each hotel property around themes that consider elements that relate to a location's history, art, culture and local businesses.

In 1993, Sondland married Katherine Durant who operated

her own holding company of shopping centers and commercial properties. She official replaced him as CEO of Provenance Hotel upon his nomination as ambassador in 2018.

Sondland and Durant have an extended history of political involvement and charitable cause donations. Although a wavering Trump supporter during the 2016 presidential election, he was reputed to have donated $1 million to Trump's Presidential Inaugural Committee motivating his ambassadorship nomination. Sondland received bipartisan support and was easily confirmed.

Sondland's brief global recognition raised his exposure into numerous media biographical profiles, examinations of his operations and the revelation of past-accused indiscretions to a wider audience. In November 2019 following his testimony, three women re-accused him of sexual misconduct and due to their refusal of his overtures resulting retaliation in the form of withdrawn investments. Upon Trump's official impeachment by the U.S. House of Representatives, Sondland's profile receded from public view.

He remained the U.S. Ambassador to the European Union to the endearment of neither political party until February 2020. Shortly after Trump was acquitted by the US. Senate along partisan voting lines, Sondland was relieved of his diplomatic duties. While Trump proponents trumpeted the acquittal as a major victory, most observers characterized it as just another cork plug temporarily suppressing a leaking and descending presidential administration. Sondland returned to the Pacific Northwest to publish a book in October 2022, his asset portfolio and renewed anonymity.

Hotel deLuxe
729 SW Fifteenth Avenue, Portland

Sentinel Hotel
614 SW Eleventh Avenue, Portland

Heathman Hotel
1001 SW Broadway Street, Portland

Hotel Dossier
750 SW Alder Street, Portland

Woodlark Hotel
813 SW Alder Street, Portland

The Murder of Aaron Danielson Amidst The Chaos of Protest and Destruction

The May 2020 homicide of George Floyd in Minneapolis unleashed a sequence of corresponding violence and protest within Portland. Nightly manifestations escalated throughout the summer and autumn with the city becoming a flashpoint for confrontation. As the protests became more politicized, common ground for discussion, compromise and compatible resolution strayed distantly.

The location of the protest movement concentrated on the Mark Hatfield Federal Courthouse, but the unrest proliferated throughout the downtown. The courthouse was barricaded by fencing and patrolled by federal law enforcement officials. The originally touted cause of racial inequality and police harassment detonated into an assortment of complaints regarding legal, social and law enforcement issues. The malaise turned violent and destructive.

Downtown became a hostile terrain of boarded up windows, graffiti and flagrant demolition. With respect for centralize authority absent, extremism pervaded the void. Activist group leaders agitated their loosely organized memberships infiltrated by radical factions. Moderation and rational dialogue was shunned or simply shouted over.

When calm words fail, the threat and deployment of physical violence and firearms gains credibility and foothold. The foot soldiers of conflict are often impressionable individuals carried away by volatile emotions of impulsiveness. In a battle zone absent of discernible uniforms or identification, two lives would be abruptly terminated over perceived philosophical differences and hatred laced intolerance.

A *Trump 2020 Cruise Rally* and ultra-conservative themed demonstration staged downtown preceded the tragedy of their deaths. Over 100 cars and trucks paraded via a packed caravan on August 29th taunting participants in a neighboring George Floyd protest. Hundreds of proponents assembled creating a tense environment. The rally's objective appeared to be publicity and provocation. Confrontation between *liberal* and *conservative* elements began initially by insults. The conflict escalated into fired paintballs, pepper spray and hurled projectiles by both sides.

Aaron Danielson, 39, was a supporter of one of the caravan organizing groups called *Patriot Prayer*. His role in the event was purportedly to *provide security*. Published accounts of his activities however indicated no direct involvement with the physical skirmishes. He was reportedly armed with a loaded Glock pistol in a holster and held a can of mace and expandable metal baton.

At 8:45 p.m. unbeknownst to Danielson, he was sighted and stalked by two men from a rival organization loosely affiliated with the Antifa movement. Antifa has been characterized as a left-wing anti-fascist and anti-racist political cause. The organization is highly decentralized and composed of a variety of autonomous groups.

Their expressed philosophy is the employment of both nonviolent and violent direct action to affect radical change, rather than simply policy reforms. Their focus has frequently been likened to historical anarchist causes. They were accused of excessive measures during the Portland protests.

The two men following Danielson, ducked into the shadows of a parking garage at the intersection of SW Third Avenue and Alder Street. Danielson and a companion walked by the location unaware of their presence.

Emerging from their concealment, the pair trailed Danielson briefly before one of them, Michael Reinoehl, 48, reached into his waistband for a .38-caliber handgun. He fired two shots at Danielson. The first bullet struck his metal canister of mace. The second hit Danielson fatally in his upper right chest.

The simmering threat became realized. Witnesses identified Reinoehl shortly afterwards. He fled into the night a fugitive without being apprehended. In the days following, the founder of the *Patriot Prayer* organization cooled his fiery rhetoric and urged mourners not to seek vengeance.

Reinoehl was charged with second-degree murder and unlawful use of a weapon four days later. He was surrounded that same evening approaching his car by members of a federal law enforcement task force in Lacey, a suburb of Olympia, Washington. Accounts have differed as to what transpired. Some versions reported that Reinoehl fired 40 to 50 rounds from a semi-automatic rifle at officers. Other witnesses stated that he was unarmed. The official law enforcement report did not indicate that Reinoehl had fired on officers, but that he drew a weapon.

Reinoehl was unable to escape as police had boxed in his vehicle. Forty rounds were confirmed fired in his direction. Video footage indicated that officers attempted to perform CPR as he lay motionless on the ground. There would be no trial to provide any explanation for his earlier actions.

Blame was liberally directed for his shooting against law enforcement officials with hundreds protesting outside a Portland police station. Donald Trump labeled Reinoehl's killing *retribution*. Further federal law enforcement intervention within Portland failed to calm the frenzy of confrontation between polarized causes.

Opposing factions subsequently blamed each other for the extensive property defacement and disregard for orderly and nonviolent protest. What has become evident from the chaos is the chasm between extremes has widened. Portland is a severely fractured community. Homeless encampments have escalated throughout the city accompanied by extensive garbage heaping.

For two idealistically misguided men, their futile sacrifice resolved nothing. Positive social evolution does not advance through the barrel of firearms. This is a lesson that contemporary society has yet once again become reluctant to grasp.

TWISTED TOUR GUIDES.com

**Mark Hatfield United States Courthouse
1000 SW Third Avenue, Portland**

Parking Structure
Intersection of SW Third Avenue and Alder Street,
Portland

Murder of Aaron Danielson
Intersection of SW Third Avenue and Alder Street,
Portland

SALEM

A Pioneer Murder, Hanging and Missing Treasure

In 1824, George Beale was born in Botetourt County, Virginia and in 1843 he made his first wagon train trek to the Oregon Territory. He married his first wife Sarah in 1848, but she died seven years later. In 1852, he made a second trans-continental wagon train voyage. He married his second wife Mariah the same year that his first wife died. With her, he fathered two boys in 1857 and 1858.

Daniel Delaney arrived in Oregon in 1843 on a wagon train with several families. He departed from Tennessee where he had owned a plantation. He had difficulty selling his slaves before departure as he did not wish to break up any families by selling them to different owners. He eventually succeeded in selling them all to a single plantation manager before heading west. His five sons accompanied him and he established a settlement in Turner, Oregon just outside of Salem. His son David constructed a house nearby.

Delaney was 71 years old and considered wealthy having brought a considerable amount of money with him. He raised cattle and enjoyed entertaining and hosting guests overnight. As the Oregon Territory had no banks, settlers had no choice but to hide their money in creative locations.

George Beale was reportedly a frequent visitor to Delaney's ranch and had enjoyed his hospitality. Some accounts indicated that he had even worked for him at one time. He envied Delaney's wealth and knew that a recent cattle sale had bloated his cashflow. He spoke openly with confidants about the ease of eliminating Delaney and stealing his cash rumored to amount to $45,000-$50,000 in $20 gold pieces. Beale speculated that he knew many of the hiding locations.

Beale was genial and well liked in Salem. He operated a saloon where the Marion Hotel would be later constructed shortly afterwards and then destroyed by fire in 1971. The site is currently the Grand Hotel. Beale recruited one of his clients, George Baker who frequently became drunk at his establishment. Baker had run up a significant bill and eventually agreed to assist Beale in a planned heist of Delaney's gold. Baker had recently arrived in Salem as a butcher by trade and stirred up gossip due to his Native American wife.

At dusk on Sunday, January 9, 1865, the pair met at a watering trough near the Delaney ranch. Both blackened their faces with charred pieces of bark. Delaney had a reputation for welcoming recently freed slaves.

Baker remained at the gate while Beale knocked on the door. Delaney answered and Beale inquired as to the location of his son's house. Beale claimed at his trial that Delaney had a knife. Baker panicked and blasted him with his double-barreled shotgun. Delaney's dog launched after Beale but was hampered by being chained. Beale wounded the dog but not fatally.

Delaney struggled to his feet and pleaded with Beale to spare his life. He even offered him all of the money. Beale preferred no witnesses and shot him dead in his forehead. He presumed that they would find the treasure absent of Delaney's instructions. The killing was Salem's first officially recorded murder.

Beale then became aware of a twelve-year old witness to the shooting. A mulatto boy named Jack DeWolf had been staying with Delaney as a caretaker. He unleashed the wounded dog and barricaded himself into an adjacent room. While Beale and Baker rammed and splintered the door with a log, Jack escaped outside into the night with the dog and hid on the property. The pair remained huddled together until morning shivering from fear and the January chill.

Beale and Baker ransacked the house but reportedly only uncovered $1,900. Beale distributed $500 to Baker. Both men buried their earnings. Beale reportedly hid his in a cigar box by the side of a creek. They were confident that their disguises offered them sufficient protection. This assumption proved premature and erroneous.

The next morning, DeWolf raced to David Delaney's house and recounted the events. He may have known Beale or heard his name shouted by the dying Delaney when he recognized his killer. Within five days, Beale and Baker were arrested and jailed.

Due to reports of their hidden cache, both men easily secured legal representation. Their lawyers stressed the need for revealing the hidden gold to them in order to *bribe witnesses*. Both men were reluctant to give up their stolen proceeds. Beale confessed that his attorney eventually discovered and pocketed his $1,400. He promised his lawyer that another $30,000 was buried elsewhere and at his disposal if he earned him a successful acquittal.

The trial began on March 21, 1865. The evidence was circumstantial, but pursued based on Jack DeWolf's account. His eyewitness testimony was excluded on the grounds *he could not comprehend the nature of an oath*. The prosecution was able to substantiate his story. The sheriff had traced the movements of the killers and found Beale's hatband and bits of charred bark at the identified watering trough. The splintered door, an ax and the log used as a battering ram were discovered exactly as DeWolf had described. Even more damaging was the two men were sighted with traces of black on their faces the day following the murder. Neither could account suitably for their location on that fateful evening.

The defense attorney spoke for over four hours in vain. The two prosecutors would eventually be elected to congress. The judge implied that the pair was guilty in his instruction to the jury. They concurred and both men were sentenced to hang.

May 17, 1865 was a local holiday and festival within Salem due to the hanging. Families with their children attended the gala toting their lunches. Two large gallows were constructed. Estimates between 1,000-5,000 were in attendance, some arriving from over twenty miles away.

Beale and Baker eventually confessed to the murder, blaming each other. Their confessions were printed and sold at the spectacle. The pair were in foul moods and did not exit their temporal life gracefully. Beale attempted to spit upon William Delaney as he was led to the rope. Part of his animosity stemmed from the Delaney family's attempt to secure the stolen $1,900. He was also irritated by an order issued previously by one of the Delaney's to the sheriff to arrest Beale for renting a billiard table previously to someone for twenty-five cents.

Once the two men were confirmed dead, the location of their burial became problematic. The local cemetery would not accept them. One of the men who'd accompanied the elder Delaney on his wagon train voyage volunteered claiming he had no religious scruples or affiliations. He loaded both cadavers on a lumber wagon, steered them onto the hills of his property and gave each a proper burial on a knoll. The location was plowed over during the 1940s.

As to the hidden riches from the Delaney estate, David Delaney could only account for $24,000 that he had discovered in a granary on the farm. He estimated that another $45,000 remained hidden. Later property owners and curious individuals have scoured inside and underneath the house, the fireplace and throughout the property. Dreamers, psychics, dowsing sticks and divining rods have been employed to no avail. Daniel Delaney's treasure (if it existed) has successfully eluded detection for over 150 years.

Salem's hanging grounds were located southeast of the downtown core on the southern bank of Pringle Creek. The adjacent Pringle Park is full of mature trees, some potentially dating from the execution day. The grounds are currently adjacent to Salem's Medical Center. At least four recorded hangings were historically conducted on the site.

The original farmhouse has miraculously survived time, decay and inclement weather. It remains one of the three oldest standing houses recognized in Oregon. The house was originally located approximately 300 feet west of its present site, but relocated to a new foundation for preservation purposes and easier street access. Additions to the structure in 1870 include a parlor, wrap-around porch and kitchen. A woodshed was added in the 1900s. The property has been renamed the Delaney House Inn offering accommodations. Treasure hunting is discouraged.

Delaney House
4292 Delaney Road SE, Salem

Salem Hanging Grounds
Pringle Park
606 Church Street SE, Salem

A Tale of Two Figures in 1890s Oregon Soiled Politics

Late nineteenth century Portland and Oregon political elections were seedy and blatantly filthy. Mired in the midst of candidate maneuvering and voter fraud was cocky transplant Jonathan Bourne Jr.

Bourne arrived in Portland in 1885 following a detoured shipwreck in Hong Kong of one of his father's whaling ships. His father also owned a clothing manufacturing business in New Bedford, Massachusetts. Portland appealed to Bourne due to its wide-open nature. Soon he had accumulated a dubious collection of friends and acquaintances amidst local hard-core vice and boardinghouse operators based in the North End.

Bourne exploited a stream of traditionally ignored voters including transient loggers, sailors, gamblers, hookers and barflies during the 1896 election. Their votes were easily obtained and collective numbers proved effective. By stuffing the North End's ballot boxes, he was able to elect himself and additionally numerous allies into Oregon's House of Representatives.

The Oregon House during that era determined the state's selections into the U.S. Senate. Bourne had secured a sufficient majority of written pledges of support for incumbent John H. Mitchell to insure his re-election. The process for obtaining their written commitment involved trading a legislator's pledge for a significant campaign contribution underwritten by the Southern Pacific Railroad.

Bourne delivered his commitment to Mitchell's re-election effort when he learned he'd been double-crossed. Rumor circulated that Mitchell planned to abandon his support of the silver standard backing U.S. currency and change his allegiance to gold. This news was potentially devastating to Bourne. He owned several Western silver mines and was passionately committed to the silver standard.

When he confronted Mitchell directly regarding his modified position, the switch was confirmed. Mitchell reminded Bourne that the pledges supporting his candidature were secure in the Southern Pacific Railroad safe and his re-election was certain.

The devious Mitchell whose life and law practice followed a chronology of bigamy, fraud and embezzlement, underestimated Bourne's cunning and loophole sniffing abilities. While it was accurate that he had sufficient votes once the legislature convened and voted in Salem's State Capitol, they had yet to assemble.

And so they didn't.

Bourne staged a decadent forty-day and forty-night party in Salem's recently completed Eldridge Block building. Bourne orchestrated the fundraising for the event including donations and entertainment from his North End vice industry supporters. Bourne made certain that his silver supporting legislators were entertained, fed and sexually preoccupied. The Oregon legislature was unable to meet with a necessary quorum. State Senator George C. Brownell of Oregon City noted with disgust that Bourne's party *was kept drunk and intoxicated for days*.

Bourne calculated that if the legislature didn't meet and vote by Inauguration Day, Oregon's Governor Lord would be obliged to appoint a Senator. Lord was a Bourne collaborator. This sequence of events transpired and another of Bourne's closest allies, Henry Corbett was appointed to the Senate in lieu of Mitchell.

Repercussions from Bourne's legislative delay were swift. The Eldridge Block was labeled *Bourne's Harem* as well as the *Den of Prostitution and Evil*. The U.S. Senate refused to seat Corbett and Oregon's second Senate position remained vacant for two years. In 1898, another close associate of Bourne, Joseph Simon was appointed by the legislature to Mitchell's former post.

It is difficult to determine which man enjoyed the best revenge amongst their intertwining destinies. In 1900, the Gold Standard Act established gold instead of silver as the only criterion for redeeming paper money. Mitchell would be voted back into the Senate in 1901, but would be indicted and convicted in 1905 of a land fraud scandal. Mitchell had used his political influence with the federal government to assist private clients with their land claims. He was never sentenced nor did he complete his Senate term.

The Senate began proceedings to expel him when unforeseen fate intervened. He died in December 1905 at the age of seventy in Portland from complications involving a tooth extraction. In 1906, Bourne would replace him becoming the first Oregon Senator to be elected by direct popular vote. He died in 1940.

Eldridge Block Building
248-254 Commercial Street NE, Salem

A History of Cruelties and Institutional Abuse Razed and Reinvented

A still standing water tower and four former grain silos are all that remain from the former Fairview Training Center, a state-run facility for individuals with developmental disabilities. The labeling has softened since Fairview was first established in 1907 as the *Oregon Institution for the Feeble-Minded*. The facility underwent three name changes during its history: Oregon Fairview Home (1933), Fairview Hospital and Training Center (1965) and the Fairview Training Center (1979).

The pertinent question remained throughout its existence, what were the inmates being trained for?

In 1908, the first patients were transferred from the Oregon State Insane Asylum (now Oregon State Hospital). They resided on a 670-acre complex consisting of an administration building called the LeBreton Cottage, a dormitory, laundry and boiler house. Five years later, two additional cottages were constructed.

The operation became a working farm offering sustenance and agricultural training for residents. Four hundred acres were cleared for orchards and crops and the farm raised hogs, chickens and cattle.

One of the most controversial requirements for the initial 300 residents beginning in 1923 was that each had to be sterilized in order to qualify for parole in the future. By 1929, the process was complete either by the patient's consent or a court order. During Fairview's existence, more than 2,600 forced sterilizations took place including vasectomies, forced hysterectomies, tubal ligations and even castrations. The state of Oregon issued a formal apology in 2002 for these excessive human rights violations.

The documented discipline tactics and punishments were despicable including razor straps, closeting, brutal spankings and scalding hot water drenching. Leather cuffs, helmets, handcuffs, straightjackets and extreme dosages of sedatives were commonly employed. Deaths from unnatural causes attributed to these abuses occurred.

The horrors eventually triggered the attention of the U.S. Department of Justice and federal funding was abruptly cut off. Advocacy groups and governmental personnel developed a long-term plan to permanently close the facility. In March 2000, the Fairview Training Center ceased operations. The property was sold to private ownership with fresh directional uses proposed. An arson fire destroyed Pierce Cottage, one of the remaining cottages in 2010. The remaining structures were demolished in 2018.

At present the landscape is being reshaped for residential habitation. Sidewalks, paving, water, sewer lines and electricity infrastructure are being installed to accommodate upcoming rental housing and development projects. The standing water tower and silos are doomed relics presumably awaiting eventual elimination. Their symbolic removal may hopefully eradicate somber memories from a darker era.

The Fairview Training Center facility is a memory most locals were ignorant about and/or would prefer to forget. The facility while in operation cultivated a reputation for haunting and paranormal activity. Considering its cruel and macabre history, such phenomenon becomes understandable. Will its fresh reinvention appease its prior demons?

**Former Fairview Training Center
Corner Property of Fairview Industrial Drive SE and
Reed Road SE, Salem**

Atmospheric Spirits and a Reborn Theatre

Salem's downtown Elsinore Theatre was constructed in 1926 with the expressed objective of resembling the castle in the Danish city of Elsinore from William Shakespeare's play *Hamlet*. Ellis F. Lawrence, the first dean from the University of Oregon's school of architecture, designed the Tudor Gothic style theatre incorporating various external and internal atmospheric themes.

The exterior is composed of cement, steel and 30-foot faux stucco stone walls. The roof is composed of layered asphalt. There is a tall rectangular center with two square attachments. The top middle section features two levels and an intriguing crown. Each of the two levels feature three windows and ornate trim. The apex of the building features the appearance of six mounted swords embedded into the structure. The Povey Brothers created the numerous stain glass windows. The upper balcony windows above the theatre entrance were transported from a German cathedral that was bombed during World War I.

The interior is equally stunning accommodating seating for 1,450 and features a 30x60' stage with phenomenal acoustics. There are two carpeted grand staircases with wrought iron railings and two expansive hand-painted Shakespearian themed murals. A large Wurlitzer organ accentuates the grandeur.

The Elsinore was originally designed for live theatre performances and silent films. Owner George Guthrie leased the theatre to Fox West Coast and Warner Brothers Theatres to show motion pictures until 1951.

By 1954, the structure began a slow decline that nearly culminated in a 1980 demolition. Preservation efforts blocked the wrecking ball and ultimately restored the gem to its former luster.

What has also distinguished the Elsinore is the level of paranormal activity reported over the decades. Original owner George Guthrie's shadowy apparition has been cited on numerous occasions by stage managers and theatre personnel. Two unsettling stories, absent of archival newspaper evidence claim a boy was murdered inside the men's bathroom periodically leaving bloody splatters and handprints on the mirror. Another involves the small daughter of one of the theatre managers falling from the balcony where she was playing. There are speculations that she may have been pushed.

The Elsinore Theatre has resumed offering concerts, theatre and live entertainment. It remains one of the choicest venues in Oregon's capital city even if patrons are obliged to share the space potentially with spirits.

Elsinore Theatre, 170 High Street SE, Salem

Abrupt Mass Death Within An Atmosphere of Institutional Discretion

Since it's founding in 1883, the Oregon State Hospital located in the historic Kirkbride Building has sometimes resembled a veritable house of horrors for mental illness patients. Originally named the *Oregon Hospital for the Insane*, the facility was actively operational in the controversial fields of electroshock therapy, lobotomies, sterilizations and hydrotherapy. These treatment extremes often ranged from barbaric excess to indifferent neglect. The institutional name was modified in 1913 to the current *Oregon State Hospital*.

In the early years, the most commonly reported causes for insanity and hospital admission were epilepsy, alcoholism, masturbation, and religious paranoia. The ratio of male to female patients was two to one.

The Salem facility was an appropriate site and setting for filming the movie *One Flew Over the Cuckoos Nest*. However the location was not the inspiration for the original novel. Author Ken Kesey worked as an evening nurse's aide in the psychiatric ward of the Menlo Park Veteran's Hospital while attending Stanford University as a creative writing student. His experiences and impressions formed the basis for his classic. During the same period, he also volunteered for CIA-financed experiments as a user with hallucinogens.

As ruthless and excessive as treatments may appear today, the worst scandal to plague the institution occurred the evening of November 18, 1942 during dinner service. At the time, the hospital housed 2,700 patients, more than five times today's population.

A batch of poisoned scrambled eggs afflicted diners immediately. Patients collapsed, vomiting blood and contorted on the floor in agony. Many were struggling to breathe and incurring seizures while some even experienced paralysis. Some died instantly, others would expire hours later. The death toll reached 47 patients. Officially 263 cases of food poisoning were recorded. Newspaper accounts reported in excess of 400 people affected. The eggs reportedly had a salty or soapy taste.

The source of the tainted eggs originated from federal surplus commodities that had been distributed to the institution, schools and other state programs six months earlier. They were packed frozen in 30-pound tin cans. Oregon governor Charles Spague labeled the poisoning *mass murder* and demanded that the institutions cease immediately using the eggs. As it turned out however, the eggs were not to blame.

A follow-up investigation revealed the poison to be sodium fluoride commonly used in insecticides and in rat and cockroach poisons. The quick acting white substance was mistakenly given to an assistant cook by a patient sent down to the basement to retrieve powdered milk. The powder was mixed into the scrambled eggs creating the lethal contamination.

Five days after the fatal dinner, two cooks were arrested and charged with involuntary manslaughter. The charges were ultimately dismissed against both. Much of the blame fell on the hospital administration for failure to follow safety measures due to gross understaffing. Reforms in food safety and labeling followed.

One of the cooks remained at the hospital in his position afterwards. The other's follow-up history was never recorded. The patient responsible for unintentionally supplying the poison lived until 1983, dying following an altercation at the institution. His death was attributed to heart disease. For the rest of his lifelong internment, he was blamed for the poisoning by patients resulting in numerous fistfights.

The Oregon State Hospital operates a self-guided museum tour documenting the history of the institution including photographs, documents, equipment and examples of restraining devices used upon patients. The presentation is candid and often unvarnished exposing sad truths regarding a forgotten population.

The most intriguing aspect of the hospital grounds is a labyrinth of subterranean tunnels and a narrow gauge railroad that were established during the initial construction. These tunnels allowed the hospital to transport patients and supplies between buildings absent of public observation. Scandalous sexual trysts between patients and employees were rumored to have occurred within these cloistered spaces. These stories remain hearsay. Many of the tunnels have reportedly been filled in due to safety concerns and access is completely off-limits to the visiting public.

Within an institutional universe of necessitated discretion and secrets, the magnitude of potential scandal and vice will never fully be revealed to the scrutiny of an uncaring outside society.

Oregon State Hospital
2600 Center Street NE, Salem

Richard Marquette: A Still Living Relic From A Costly Early Release Blunder

On the evening of June 6, 1961, Joan Caudie was drinking alone at a Portland bar when she noticed an elementary school classmate, Richard Marquette. She approached him and over continued drinks, the 24-year-old married mother of two and Marquette caught up on the narrative of their lives since school days.

Marquette regularly trawled local bars and boasted that he could consume three-fourths of a case of beer and still walk. He was a driver for Hodes Auto Wrecking Yard, now defunct. Throughout that extended June evening, they drank, stumbled to more taverns, drank excessively and reportedly even crossed the Hawthorne Bridge before arriving via taxi to his southeastern Portland apartment.

Perhaps he envisioned a sexual consummation following extended kissing in the cab. Perhaps they quarreled later over an insignificant disagreement. He conveniently claimed to investigators that he was *dead drunk* and remembered nothing. He awoke the next morning to discover Caudie's corpse in his residence strangled.

Marquette did the only sensible act a deranged serial killer might consider. Her carried her body into his bathroom shower stall and cut it into pieces. A week later, portions of the now missing woman would be found in a cardboard box propped against an Alder Street garage door. The container included two of her fingers and other internal organs. Further components of the corpse had been wrapped in newspaper and deposited near SE Fifteenth Avenue and Oak Street. Leaving investigators no doubt as to the responsible party, additional parts were stuffed in a duffel bag in Marquette's refrigerator. Her head was never recovered.

For three weeks, Marquette fled Portland taking buses and hitchhiking throughout the Western United States and Mexico. He was added to the FBI's Most Wanted list. He was eventually tracked down and arrested without resistance at a Santa Maria, California salvage yard where he was temporarily employed.

Marquette was convicted of first-degree murder and sentenced to life imprisonment. He was interned at the Oregon State Penitentiary where he remained forgotten and a model prisoner. After serving only twelve years, he was paroled.

Prison existence is not the same as adaptation to the outside world. The Oregon prison system has a historically deplorable record of releasing perpetrators of murder and even serial killers prematurely. The clearly mentally disturbed Marquette would have never been adaptable.

He was given a second opportunity to kill and even dismember. He took full advantage.

Following his release, he became a plumber's helper in Salem with the assistance of his parole officer. He resided in a trailer park that still operates. Twenty-seven months after prison, he strangled 35-year-old Betty Lucille Wilson and dismembered her body. He dumped her in a Willamette River slough. He confessed to investigators that he had killed and dismembered another woman since his release. He even reportedly led them to some of her remains. She has never been publicly identified.

Richard Lawrence Marquette is 88-years-old and currently an inmate at the Oregon State Correctional Institution since

2005. He was imprisoned in various facilities outside of Oregon for a decade due to his notoriety. This internment has been characterized by continued good behavior, involvement with prison veterans and Catholic groups and his sorting of cardboard, plastics and other garbage for the prison's recycling program.

Forty-five years since his earlier idiotic release have passed. The only positive result is that concrete legislative efforts have been initiated to tighten parole eligibility for first-degree murder convicts. For two women and potentially more, this flaw in common sense resulted in their needless gruesome deaths.

Richard Marquette's Salem Residence
Highway Avenue Trailer Park
1865 Highway Avenue, Salem

Women's Shoe Fetish Killer Plagues the Willamette Valley

In the tormented existence of serial killer Jerry Brudos, fetish for women's shoes began at the age of five. His mother had wanted a daughter and reportedly despised and belittled him. His teen years were marred by sexual fantasies fueled by his hatred towards women and a desire for revenge against his mother. He fulfilled these obsessions with violence towards women. Periodically he stole their shoes afterwards.

He graduated from high school despite being institutionalized for nine months in a psychiatric ward at the Oregon State Hospital. He found employment afterwards as an electronic engineer assuming a more conventional lifestyle by marrying and settling in a Portland suburb.

Concurrently, he began suffering severe migraine headaches and reportedly began night prowling raids to steal women's shoes and lace undergarments. By the end of the decade, his symptoms escalated and his attempts to curb his mania turned lethal.

Between January 1968 and April 1969, Brudos was responsible for killing four women and a botched abduction. Three of the murders were committed in the Salem area where he had relocated residence.

On May 10th and 12th, 1969, the bodies of victims Linda Salee (22) and Karen Elena Sprinker (19) were found respectively weighted down by automotive parts in the Long Tom River near Monroe. On July 27, 1969, a third victim, Jan Whitney was found tied to a piece of railroad iron in the Willamette River near Independence. His fourth victim, Linda Swanson's body was never recovered. Brudos confessed that he had thrown her body into the Willamette River from the Wilsonville Bridge off Interstate 5.

Brudos tactics with three of his victims involved either offering emergency assistance or dressing up in a uniform and badge and kidnapping them. They were strangled shortly afterwards. He transported each unconscious or deceased into his home garage where he toyed and raped the cadavers. He photographed the women as they expired and/or following death. He preserved body parts as trophies. He reportedly dressed in women's underwear and footwear and masturbated afterwards.

Karen Sprinker's killing ultimately proved to be Brudos' downfall as he brazenly began telephoning her roommates following her death. Brudos claimed to be a Vietnam veteran looking for a date. One of them actually went out with him once, but found the encounter very uncomfortable. Police officers convinced her to arrange another date with Brudos. When he arrived to pick her up, a team of police officers was waiting.

During his interrogation over the following week, Brudos confessed to all four murders and the attempted abduction. Having been identified by his potential abduction victim, police obtained a search warrant for Brudos' home. There they made the gruesome discovery of nylon rope, photographs of the dead women and the physical trophies he had kept.

At trial, he was found guilty for the murders of Sprinkler, Whitney and Salee and sentenced to three consecutive life sentences. He was not charged with the fourth killing since a body had never been recovered.

He was interned in the Oregon State Penitentiary for thirty-seven years before his death in March 2006. In an interview conducted a year before his death, Brudos indicated that he had survived a recent bout of colon cancer surgery and had earned two university degrees in general science and counseling while incarcerated. During his imprisonment, he accumulated piles of women's shoe catalogs in his cell. He had written major shoe companies requesting them claiming they served as a substitute for pornography.

In 1995, the Oregon parole review board informed him that he would never be released on parole within his lifetime, a judgment Brudos found *an act of vengeance*. Brudos confessed that *he accepted responsibility for his crimes but preferred not to dwell on what happened*.

The dark duality of Jerry Brudos eluded those closest to him. When he was arrested for the murders at the age of thirty, his friends described him as a *mild-mannered devoted family man of two children, who neither drank nor smoked and rarely if ever used profanity*.

Shortly after his guilty plea, his 25-year old wife Ralphene was tried as an accomplice to her husband's murders. In October 1969, a jury acquitted her of first-degree murder charges. Illustrating the depth of his depravity, Jerry Brudos claimed that she had convinced him to sign the confessions to protect her and their children. She divorced him, changed her name and left Oregon with their children.

Reportedly none of his family members were allowed entrance into his garage according to his wife. The sole relief to society is that Brudos was captured promptly before he accumulated even more victims.

Karen Sprinker's Abduction Location:
City Center Parking Lot (Rooftop Level)
465 Church Street NE, Salem

Jerry Brudos' Former Residence
707 Edina Lane NE, Salem

A Murder Within Law Enforcement Ranks

Tuesday, November 25, 1975 appeared to be a routine workday for Holly Holcomb, the Superintendent of the Oregon State Police. He was completing his ninth year as Superintendent and the Thanksgiving holiday was only two days away. Holcomb rode into work with his deputy Bryon Hazelton. Hazelton parked in front of the Public Service Building and the pair walked towards the entrance.

En route, they were approached by Robert Wampler who shook hands and began conversing with Holcomb. Hazelton continued towards the building.

Wampler and Holcomb were very familiar with each other. Wampler had joined the Oregon State Police in 1940 but left in 1953 to become a special agent in charge of the National Automobile Theft Bureau for Oregon. He rejoined the state police in 1956. Two years later, Wampler was fired for *insubordination and conduct unbecoming the agency* prompted by disciplinary charges initiated by Holcomb then a lieutenant in Milwaukie. For seventeen years both men had remained on uneasy terms as Wampler sought to rehabilitate his name and reputation by disputing the charges all the way to the Oregon Supreme Court. In 1962, Wampler ran unsuccessfully for governor against Mark Hatfield and Robert Thornton.

During the course of their conversation Wampler became agitated. He pulled out a .38-caliber pistol and fired two shots into Holcomb's chest and abdomen. One of the shots pierced his aorta and he died less than two hours later.

Wampler was arrested within minutes of the shooting and charged with murder. He pled *insanity by reason of mental defect* during his three-week trial, but was convicted and sentenced to life imprisonment. He was released in November 1983 after serving less than eight years, considered by many a far greater injustice than the killing. He died in 1997.

Holly Holcomb's name is engraved on the Oregon State Police Fallen Trooper Memorial established close to his crime site. Thirty-three officers and troopers are currently commemorated on the monument walls. None except Holcomb were senselessly gunned down by one of their own former peers.

Holly Holcomb's Murder Site

Oregon State Police Fallen Trooper Memorial
Oregon State Police Department
255 Capitol Street NE, Salem

William Scott Smith: A Pathetic and Pitch Darkened Predator

Eighteen-year old Sherry Eyerly wasn't scheduled to work the evening of July 4, 1982. She was called in on short notice to make pizza deliveries. At approximately 9:30 p.m., she was sent out on an order to a remote periphery of West Salem near the convergence of Riverhaven Drive South and Brown Island Road.

Then as now, the rural stretch near the bend of the Willamette River is somber, isolated and foreboding. Few residential properties are located nearby. The order that she was delivering had intentionally been placed from a hotel to a non-existent address.

Later that evening, her Domino's delivery truck was found empty with the engine still running. Sherry's hat was discovered near the van along with three pizza boxes and evidence of a physical struggle. There was no trace of Sherry.

The following day, a ransom demand was phoned into the Domino's outlet. No further communications followed or efforts made to collect any money.

Initially police pursued a suspicious lead phoned in by a Salem woman. Her tip pointed towards her brother-in-law's involvement. She claimed that he had a drug problem and had mysteriously repainted his truck a different color the day after Eyerly's disappearance. His interview with police went poorly due to his nervousness and evasiveness. He couldn't adequately account for his whereabouts on the evening of Sherry's disappearance. He denied emphatically knowing her or having anything to do with harming her.

Desperate for clues and motive, police began working with a psychic investigator. The psychic implicated the suspect completely absent of evidence and based on a sequence of visions. Hours following the psychic's public pronouncement of guilt, the suspect committed suicide. Based on this strange sequence, many observers felt Sherry's case was solved and the suicide had confirmed his guilt.

They were incorrect.

Almost two years later on April 7, 1984, a similar murder occurred involving 18-year old Katie Redmond after leaving a college fraternity party at approximately 2 a.m. Her borrowed vehicle was discovered with the motor still running, the door open and signs of a struggle. Redmond was found four days later nude along Little Pudding River, just outside of Salem. Death was induced by asphyxiation.

Her killer, William Scott Smith made his most pronounced error when his distinctive late-1960s Pontiac station wagon was sighted in the area where Redmond's car was recovered. Eyewitnesses viewed his vehicle at the same approximate time that she was estimated to have met her abductor. Police had not yet connected Redmond's murder with Sherry Eyerly's. However, they did compare the similarities with the abduction and strangulation of 21-year old Rebecca Darling two months earlier.

On February 19th, Darling had disappeared from her graveyard shift job at an all-night convenience store. She had serviced a client at around 3:20 a.m. but went missing thirty minutes later when a subsequent customer arrived to discover the store deserted. Her body had been found in shrubbery adjacent to Little Pudding River two weeks before Katie Redmond's murder. She was nude from the waist up, had been raped with her hands bound behind her back and then strangled to death by a piece of rope.

Smith made the case against him for two homicides traceable and almost too simplistic. During the early morning hours of Redmond's abduction, he had telephoned a tow truck to rescue him from a ditch near the location where her car was later found. Detectives had no trouble locating him for questioning. He had been incarcerated for 180 days after pleading guilty to a series of obscene and threatening phone calls.

On April 26, 1984, Smith was arraigned on two counts of first-degree murder for the killings of Redmond and Darling. Waving a jury trial, he was convicted on both counts by a presiding judge and sentenced to two consecutive terms of life imprisonment.

For twenty years, the mystery behind Sherry Eyerly's disappearance remained unresolved with only Smith the most presumable suspect. In the current era of cold case investigations, detectives returned to their former sources and leads to determine if anything had been overlooked. Smith had been previously questioned regarding Eyerly's disappearance but his alibi had located him hundreds of miles from Salem.

The alibi fractured when investigators learned he had indeed been stopped and questioned by the police near the crime scene within hours of her original disappearance. This critical detail renewed their hopes in uncovering the truth.

Life imprisoned felons have endless hours at their disposal. Smith would not be eligible for parole until he had served at least forty years. Convicts often boast about their criminal exploits and excesses, particularly amongst their cellmates. Two prisoners indicated that Smith had admitted being involved previously with a *pizza girl*. Not only had he spoken regarding the subject, but indiscreetly while he was being secretly recorded. The prisoners offered his confession on a cassette tape as a bartering medium for their own behalf to police.

Armed with new evidence, investigators approached an uncooperative Smith. With few prospects of ever leaving prison while living, the only incentive they could offer was relocating him to another penal institution. He agreed to the offer and then confessed Eyerly's murder details.

Smith claimed the abduction was intended for one of Sherry's coworkers. The setup was conducted with his *good friend* Roger who had conveniently just died a few months previously. Roger ordered the pizzas and when the delivery truck arrived, Smith flagged Eyerly down. When she got out to retrieve the pizzas, the pair forcibly dragged her into Roger's truck.

After violating her, Smith strangled her to death and dumped the body presumably into his preferential Little Pudding River. The story corroborated the crime scene. After twenty-five years immersed in water, there would exist no remains of Sherry Eyerly to discover. A third life sentence would be added to his previous two.

Smith's highway to homicide was littered with red flags. He was a high school dropout and habitually unemployed. His official criminal career began in 1978 with a charge of *menacing* in Silverton, Oregon. The same year, a second-degree burglary charge earned him a one-year suspended sentence.

In 1979, he and a companion were accused of second-degree assault on a female victim. His companion was incarcerated and Smith acquitted. He was convicted of *indecent exposure* in Boise, Idaho in 1981. The following year, he became a suspect of interest in the unsolved murder of 14-year old Lisa Chambers.

Given the trajectory his life was heading, it is not difficult to assume his three convicted murders were not his sole homicides. The only question regarding William Scott Smith was *when* his brazen ineptness would ultimately enable his capture and conviction.

Smith is currently rotting away institutionalized from public scrutiny. He will hopefully die in prison cursed and despised. A weathering memorial cross for Sherry Eyerly adorns Brown Island Road near the fatal juncture where her life was abruptly abbreviated.

Abduction Site of Sherry Eyerly
Riverhaven Drive S near Brown Island Road, Salem

Sherry Eyerly Memorial Cross
Brown Island Road, Salem

Michael Francke's Stabbing: A Disturbing Murder and Requiem

At the conclusion of the workday, Tuesday evening January 17, 1989 around 6:45 p.m., staff members from the Oregon Department of Corrections sighted director Michael Francke within the department headquarters. Forty minutes later, two senior staff members discovered Francke's car parked in his designated spot with the driver's side door open. The car was then secured and locked, but where was the owner?

Security was notified regarding this strange occurrence and for several subsequent hours a coordinated search was conducted throughout the building. The whereabouts of Francke remained a mystery. There was no evidence of foul play or violence. Local police were not summoned to investigate.

Those involved in the search presumed that perhaps Francke had attended an event or dinner engagement and absentmindedly neglected to close the door.

Early the next morning, Francke's body was discovered sprawled on the pavement outside the department headquarters in a pool of his blood. His autopsy revealed that he had been stabbed to death the evening before.

Theories abounded as to the cause and motive for his death. Nearly twenty months before, he had been hired away from New Mexico's Department of Corrections (DOC) to become Oregon's DOC director. His mandate was to modernize and expand Oregon's prison system. Conditions were considered overcrowded and there were suspicions of corruption within the system hierarchy.

An outside reformer is rarely welcomed anywhere. Francke met immediate resistance from existing and entrenched forces. He faced criticism for cost overruns and delays in prison construction programs by legislative voices. There were plenty of potential candidates who might want him eliminated. However, there were neither confirmed linkages nor even a murder weapon.

Fifteen months later, a small-scale methamphetamine dealer, Frank Gable, was arrested and charged with the murder. His motive was explained as a car burglary gone homicidal. Francke's missing body during the crucial evening hours proved more problematic to explain.

At Gable's trial, the prosecution paraded a string of criminal associates to testify citing his confession in their presence of the crime. A teenage runaway confirmed that she viewed the murder, but later recounted her testimony and claimed another local drug dealer was responsible. No physical evidence was produced directly linking Gable to the crime.

The hearsay evidence proved sufficient for a jury to convict Gable on six counts of aggravated murder. On June 27, 1991, he was sentenced to life in prison without the possibility of parole. Twenty-three years of incarceration passed before the Federal Public Defender's Office sought to reopen the case on appeal of a conviction based primarily on dubious testimony. During the interim years, critical newspaper evaluations and alternative suspects were introduced as probable perpetrators. An ironic majority of these candidates are now deceased. Conspiracy theories regarding prison officials actually financing the hit even circulated.

For nearly three decades since his conviction, Gable has

consistently maintained his innocence. Many of the prosecution witnesses reportedly recanted their previous testimonies. Some of these individuals claimed that they offered their false testimony because police threatened them, while others maintained they wanted to punish Gable *for being a snitch for the Kelzer Police Department*. The only certain conclusion is that the party or parties responsible remain mute and uninterested in confession.

In April 2019, a U.S. Magistrate Judge ordered the State of Oregon to retry Frank Gable or release him within 90 days. Part of his ruling stemmed from excluded evidence that pointed towards another convicted felon who reportedly later confessed to the killing.

On June 28, 2019. Gable was released from prison.

Justice for Michael Francke's murder now remains as abstract and muddled as the morning of his lifeless discovery. Was a network of corruption within the prison system responsible for his death? A rectangular welded steel memorial adorns the western entrance to the DOC's headquarters. An inscription towards the bottom is engraved *End of Watch* accompanied by the date of his death.

On the building's east entrance flank is another memorial acknowledging an opening scene from the 1975 film *One Flew Over the Cuckoo's Nest*. The pavement fronting the building entrance is where Jack Nicholson's character Randle McMurphy is dropped off for admission into a psychiatric hospital.

The resulting absurdity behind a mortally flawed crime investigation mirrors the travesty McMurphy's character is subjected to within the mental institution. Grave questions linger regarding how Francke's murder was investigated. When the director of an entire state prison system is dumped unceremoniously on the institution's doorstep, the message and symbolism seems more than coincidental.

**Oregon Department of Corrections Dome Building
2575 Center Street NE, Salem**

One Flew Over the Cuckoo's Nest Memorial Signage

Michael Francke Memorial Sculpture

Author, photographer and visual artist Marques Vickers was born in 1957 in Vallejo, California. He graduated from Azusa Pacific University in Los Angeles and became the Public Relations and Executive Director for the Burbank, California Chamber of Commerce between 1979-84.

Professionally, he has operated travel, apparel, wine, rare book and publishing businesses. His paintings and sculptures have been exhibited in art galleries, private collections and museums in the United States and Europe. He has previously lived in the Burgundy and Languedoc regions of France and currently lives in the South Puget Sound region of Western Washington.

He has written and published over one hundred books spanning a diverse variety of subjects including true crime, international travel, social satire, wine production, architecture, history, fiction, auctions, fine art, poetry and photojournalism.

He has two daughters, Charline and Caroline who reside in Europe.